Complete
Canadian
Curriculum

Grade

2

Contents Grade 2

Mathematics

1 Numbers to 20   6
2 Numbers 21 to 100   10
3 Addition of 2-Digit Numbers   14
4 Subtraction of 2-Digit Numbers   18
5 More about Addition and Subtraction   22
6 Time and Temperature   26
7 Length   30
8 Perimeter and Area   34
9 Money   38
10 Addition and Subtraction with Money   42
11 2-D Shapes (1)   46
12 2-D Shapes (2)   50
13 Symmetry   54
14 3-D Figures   58
15 Multiplication (1)   62
16 Multiplication (2)   66
17 More about Multiplication   70
18 Division   74
19 Fractions (1)   78
20 Fractions (2)   82
21 Capacity   86
22 Mass   90
23 Patterns (1)   94
24 Patterns (2)   98
25 Organizing Data   102
26 Pictographs   106
27 Bar Graphs   110
28 Probability   114

English

1 Say It with Flowers   120
2 Tongue Twisters   124
3 The Tomatina – the Strangest Festival in the World 128
4 Let's Save Water   132
5 Tooth Tales from around the World   136
6 Mmmmm...Poutine!   140
7 Kelly's Broken Wrist   144
8 Onomatopoeia   148
9 My Special Hobby   152
10 Berry Time   156
11 Who Invented the Sandwich?   160
12 Brother Moon and Sister Sun – an Inuit Legend 164
13 Chinese Birth Signs   168
14 Billy's Bad Dream   172
15 S'mores!   176
16 How Canada Got Its Name   180
17 Scotty the T. Rex   184
18 My Little Sister's Challenge   188
19 Canada's Great Polar Bear Swim   192
20 Why the Sea Is Salty   196
21 My Grandma's Special Hobby   200
22 Fluffy the Wonder Dog   204
23 A New Student in Class   208
24 A New Game   212
25 I Want to Be a...   216
26 When Grandma Was a Girl Like Me   220
27 The Fox and the Stork   224
28 Johnny Appleseed   228

Social Studies

Heritage and Identity: Changing Family and Community Traditions

1 My Family   234

2 Different Traditions and Celebrations   236

3 Traditional Foods   238

4 Our Traditions and Celebrations   240

5 Ethnic Foods and Things   242

6 Special Days   244

7 Changing Traditions   246

8 Celebrating Differently   248

9 Mapping Our Traditions   250

10 Our Thanksgiving Celebration   252

People and Environments: Global Communities

11 Our World   254

12 The Globe   256

13 Climates of North America   258

14 Unique Countries   260

15 Our Unique Country   262

16 Travel around the World   264

17 Our Basic Needs   266

18 Living around the World   268

19 Clothes and Homes   270

20 Sports and Recreation   272

21 Foods from around the World   274

22 Where People Live   276

23 Adapting to a Place   278

24 Preserving Our Resources   280

Science

1 Animals   284

2 Ways Animals Eat and Move   286

3 Animal Homes   288

4 Winter Survival   290

5 Migration   292

6 Animal Babies   294

7 Animal Growth   296

8 Life Cycles   298

9 Camouflage and Adaptation   300

10 Properties of Liquids and Solids   302

11 More about Liquids and Solids   304

12 Three States of Water   306

13 Buoyancy   308

14 Hazard Symbols   310

15 Air around Us   312

16 Water around Us   314

17 Clean Air and Water   316

18 Energy Input and Output   318

19 Energy from Moving Water and Wind   320

20 Windmills and Water Wheels   322

21 Positions   324

22 Movements   326

23 Simple Machines   328

24 Movements and Mechanisms   330

Answers

Mathematics   334

English   346

Social Studies   356

Science   362

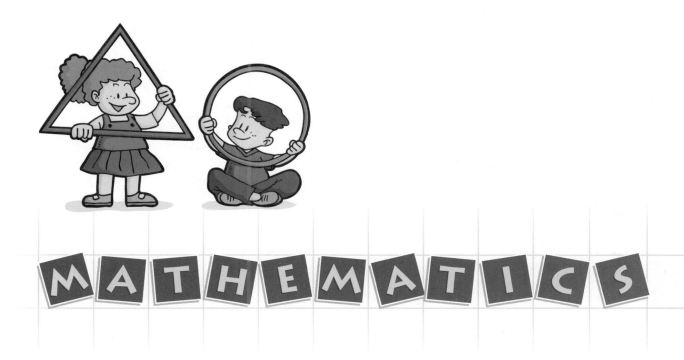

MATHEMATICS

*   The Canadian penny is no longer in circulation. It is used in the units to show money amounts to the cent.

Numbers to 20

- Count and write numbers to 20.
- Write numbers to 20 in words.
- Compare and order numbers to 20.
- Add and subtract numbers to 18.

I have twelve doughnuts.

Count and write the numbers.

①

②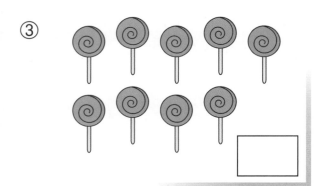

③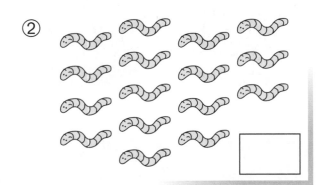

④

⑤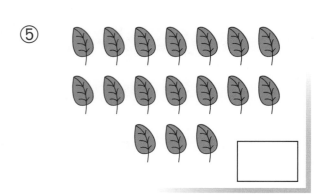

⑥

Write the numbers in words.

⑦ 14 _____

⑧ 8 _____

⑨ 16 _____

⑩ 19 _____

⑪ 20 _____

⑫ 11 _____

⑬ 7 _____

⑭ 12 _____

Complete the crossword puzzle with numbers in words.

⑮

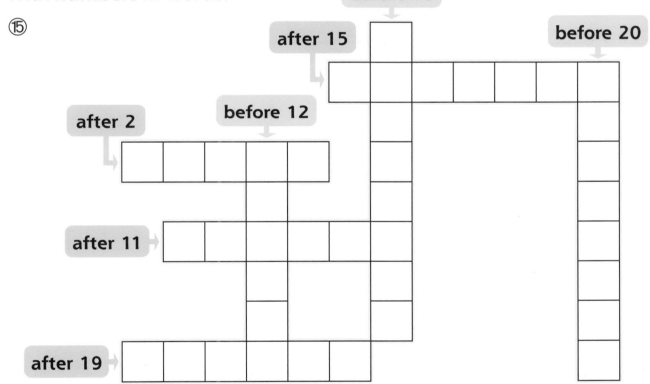

before 19

after 15

before 20

after 2

before 12

after 11

after 19

Colour the greater number.

⑯ 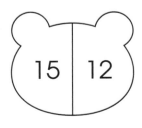 15 | 12

⑰ 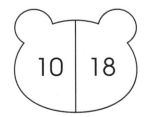 10 | 18

⑱ 6 | 11

Put the numbers in order from least to greatest.

⑲   6   5   11   10

_____

⑳   17   14   9   20

_____

㉑   15   8   13   19

_____

㉒   5   16   12   18

_____

Fill in the missing numbers.

㉓   9 ____ ____ 12 ____ ____ 15 ____ ____ 18

㉔   16 ____ 14 ____ ____ 11 ____ 9 ____ ____

㉕   11 ____ ____ 14   15 ____ ____ 18 ____ ____

Add or subtract.

㉖
$$9$$
$$+ \quad 3$$

㉗
$$15$$
$$- \quad 8$$

㉘
$$11$$
$$- \quad 6$$

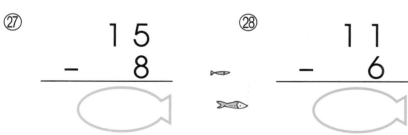

㉙   8 + 8 = ____

㉚   10 – 9 = ____

㉛   7 + 4 = ____

㉜   12 – 7 = ____

㉝   17 – 9 = ____

㉞   5 + 6 = ____

Some words tell whether you should add or subtract.

- Clue words for **addition**:
  more...than; add; sum; in all; total; together; both

- Clue words for **subtraction**:
  less...than; fewer; take away; remains; have left; are left

Underline the clue words in the questions. Then solve the problems.

③⑤ David has 7 green marbles and 5 red marbles. How many marbles does he have in all?

_____ marbles

③⑥ Ted has 16 robots. If he gives 9 to David, how many robots will he have left?

_____ robots

③⑦ Jason has 4 more stickers than Nancy. If Nancy has 9 stickers, how many stickers does Jason have?

_____ stickers

③⑧ Jane has 12 doughnuts. If I eat 8 doughnuts, how many doughnuts will she have left?

_____ doughnuts

Numbers 21 to 100

- Count and write numbers to 100.
- Compare and order numbers to 100.
- Count by 1's, 2's, 5's, 10's, and 25's.
- Identify the value of a digit in a 2-digit number.

2 is in the tens place and 0 is in the ones place. I can have twenty lollipops.

2 is in the ones place. I have two lollipops only.

Count and write the numbers.

①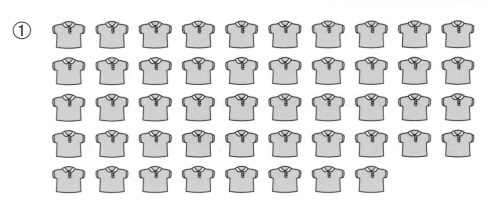

②

Colour the smaller number.

③  15 33

④  24 19

⑤ 82 78

⑥ 65 56

Put the numbers in order from greatest to least.

⑦   42   57   60   49   _____

⑧   84   68   48   80   _____

⑨   35   50   53   33   _____

Circle the items. Then fill in the blanks.

⑩   Circle by 2's.

a. There are _____ 2's.

b. There are _____ light bulbs in all.

⑪   Circle by 5's.

a. There are _____ 5's.

b. There are _____ screws in all.

Count by 1's, 2's, 5's, 10's, or 25's to find out the value in each group.

⑫

_____ ¢ in all

⑬

_____ ¢ in all

⑭

_____ ¢ in all

⑮

_____ ¢ in all

⑯

_____ ¢ in all

⑰

_____ ¢ in all

Fill in the missing numbers.

⑱ 5   10   15   25   30   45

⑲ 10   20   40   60   70   80

⑳ 46   48      54   56      60   62

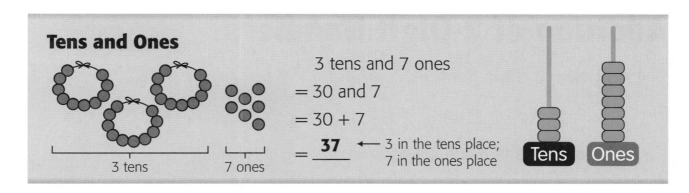

Tens and Ones

3 tens and 7 ones

= 30 and 7

= 30 + 7

= **37** ← 3 in the tens place;
7 in the ones place

3 tens   7 ones

Tens   Ones

Look at the pictures. Fill in the blanks. Then draw beads to show the numbers.

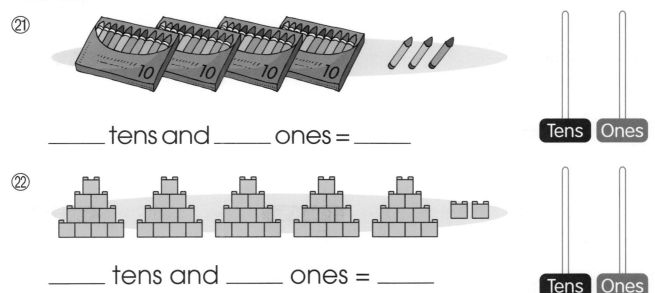

㉑

_____ tens and _____ ones = _____

Tens   Ones

㉒

_____ tens and _____ ones = _____

Tens   Ones

Fill in the blanks.

㉓ 73 = ____ tens ____ ones

㉔ ____ = 2 tens 8 ones

㉕ 65 = ____ tens ____ ones

㉖ ____ = 9 tens 1 one

Read what Jill says. Solve the problem.

㉗ *I have 3 groups of tens and 2 groups of ones. How many candies do I have in all?*

_____ candies

Addition of 2-Digit Numbers

$$\begin{array}{r} 1\ 9 \\ +\ \ 2\ 6 \\ \hline 4\ 5 \end{array}$$

- Add two 2-digit numbers without regrouping.
- Add two 2-digit numbers with regrouping.
- Solve problems involving the addition of 2-digit numbers.

I have 45 bananas.

26

19

Do the addition.

①
Tens	Ones
3	5
+ 1	2

②
Tens	Ones
4	3
+ 2	1

③
Tens	Ones
3	6
+	3

④
Tens	Ones
2	7
+ 6	2

⑤
Tens	Ones
5	3
+ 4	4

⑥
Tens	Ones
	5
+ 8	0

⑦ $34 + 51 =$ _____

⑧ $62 + 10 =$ _____

⑨ $15 + 23 =$ _____

⑩ $45 + 42 =$ _____

⑪ $20 + 18 =$ _____

⑫ $14 + 63 =$ _____

⑬ $7 + 42 \ =$ _____

⑭ $37 + 2 \ =$ _____

⑮ $61 + 11 =$ _____

⑯ $23 + 43 =$ _____

⑰ $4 + 52 \ =$ _____

⑱ $18 + 81 =$ _____

Do the addition.

⑲
```
    ◯
  3 5
+ 2 8
─────
```

⑳
```
    ◯
  4 7
+ 2 9
─────
```

㉑
```
    ◯
  1 8
+ 5 4
─────
```

㉒
```
    ◯
  4 3
+ 3 9
─────
```

㉓
```
    ◯
  2 4
+ 2 9
─────
```

㉔
```
    ◯
  6 3
+ 1 7
─────
```

㉕ 28 + 28 = _____

㉖ 45 + 39 = _____

㉗ 14 + 56 = _____

㉘ 37 + 26 = _____

Do the addition. Then colour the cat and the fish that have the same answer to see which cats have no fish.

㉙
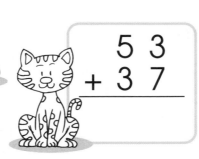
```
  2 4
+ 1 9
─────
```
```
  5 3
+ 3 7
─────
```

```
  4 8
+ 4 8
─────
```

62 + 28 = _____

25 + 16 = _____

9 + 49 = _____

33 + 8 = _____

Use an arrow to locate the number on the number line and circle the correct number. Then round the number to the nearest ten.

㉚
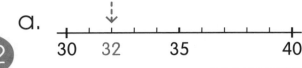

32

a.

b. 32 is closer to 30 / 40 ; 32 is rounded to _____ .

㉛
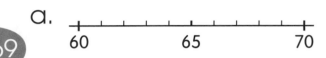

69

a.

b. 69 is closer to 60 / 70 ; 69 is rounded to _____ .

㉜

44

a.

b. 44 is closer to 40 / 50 ; 44 is rounded to _____ .

Round each number to the nearest ten to do the estimate. Then find the exact answer.

㉝

```
    3 9
  + 5 3
```

Estimate

+ _____

㉞

```
    4 8
  + 1 7
```

Estimate

_____

㉟

```
    8 1
  + 1 2
```

Estimate

_____

㊱

```
    5 9
  + 2 4
```

Estimate

_____

Look at the pictures. Answer the questions.

③⑦  14

38

How many dolls are there in all?

_____ dolls

③⑧

Lucy

I have 46 stickers.

Katie has 6 more stickers than Lucy. How many stickers does Katie have?

_____ stickers

③⑨  37¢

How much do 2 giraffes cost?

_____ ¢

④⓪

I have given 36 bananas to each of my two friends. How many bananas do my friends have in all?

_____ = _____

_____ bananas

Subtraction of 2-Digit Numbers

39 lollipops left

- Subtract 1-digit and 2-digit numbers with or without trading.
- Estimate the answer by rounding each number to the nearest ten.

Do the subtraction.

①
Tens	Ones
4	6
− 1	2

②
Tens	Ones
9	7
− 3	6

③
Tens	Ones
7	3
− 2	0

④ 84 − 31 = _____

⑤ 62 − 21 = _____

⑥ 77 − 73 = _____

⑦ 55 − 43 = _____

⑧ 68 − 56 = _____

⑨ 89 − 76 = _____

⑩ Sam has 38 candies. If he eats 15 candies, how many candies will he have left?

_____ candies

⑪ Ted has 75 cars and Tom has 12 fewer cars. How many cars does Tom have?

_____ cars

Do the subtraction.

⑫
```
  4 17
  5̶ 7̶
- 2 9
_____
```

⑬
```
  5 13
  6̶ 3̶
- 2 4
_____
```

⑭
```
  4 14
  5̶ 4̶
- 3 8
_____
```

⑮
```
  7 0
- 3 6
_____
```

⑯
```
  8 1
- 4 9
_____
```

⑰
```
  4 2
- 3 4
_____
```

⑱ 47 – 29 = _____

⑲ 84 – 66 = _____

⑳ 53 – 36 = _____

㉑ 72 – 47 = _____

㉒ 62 – 48 = _____

㉓ 34 – 16 = _____

㉔

Number of Tickets Sold

Sun: 94 tickets   Mon: 39 tickets   Tue: 46 tickets

a. How many more tickets were sold on Sunday than on Monday?

b. How many fewer tickets were sold on Monday than on Tuesday?

_____ more

_____ fewer

Use an arrow to locate each number on the number line. Circle the correct number. Then estimate and find the exact answer.

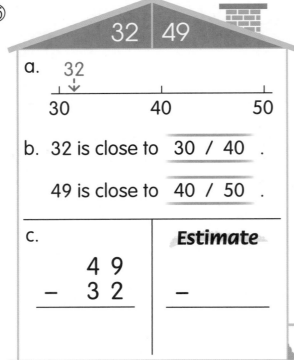

㉕

32 | 49

a. 32

30   40   50

b. 32 is close to __30 / 40__ .

     49 is close to __40 / 50__ .

c.

```
  4 9
- 3 2
```

Estimate

_−_

㉖

76 | 93

a.

70   80   90   100

b. 76 is close to __70 / 80__ .

     93 is close to __90 / 100__ .

c.

```
  9 3
- 7 6
```

Estimate

_−_

Estimate. Then find the exact answers.

㉗

Estimate

```
  4 6
- 1 8
```

㉘

Estimate

```
  7 2
- 5 4
```

㉙

Estimate

```
  5 7
- 3 3
```

㉚

Estimate

```
  8 4
- 4 9
```

Find how many gumballs are in each machine. Then answer the questions.

㉛

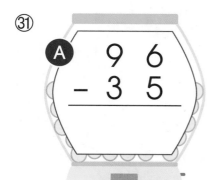
A 9 6
  − 3 5

B 7 1
  − 2 8

C 8 0
  −   4

㉜ Which machine has the most gumballs? _____

㉝ Which machine has the fewest gumballs? _____

㉞ How many more gumballs are there in **A** than in **B** ?

_____ more

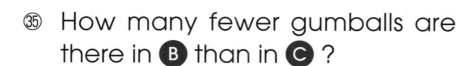

㉟ How many fewer gumballs are there in **B** than in **C** ?

_____ fewer

㊱
I have eaten 16 gumballs. How many gumballs are left?

_____ gumballs

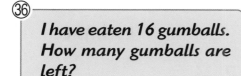

5

More about Addition and Subtraction

- Estimate the answer by rounding each number to the nearest ten.
- Use addition to check the answer of a subtraction problem.
- Understand the relationship between addition and subtraction.

Round each number to the nearest ten to estimate the answer. Then find the exact answer.

① **Estimate**

```
  4 7
+ 3 8
```

② **Estimate**

```
  6 3
- 2 5
```

③ **Estimate**

```
  5 3
- 2 9
```

④ **Estimate**

```
  1 1
+ 8 4
```

⑤ **Estimate**

```
  6 8
- 1 7
```

⑥ **Estimate**

```
  7 6
+   9
```

Use addition to check each answer. If the answer is correct, put a check mark ✔ in the fish; otherwise, put a cross ✗ and write the correct answer.

⑦

$$\begin{array}{r} 9\ 5 \\ -\ 6\ 3 \\ \hline 3\ 2 \end{array}$$

Check

$$\begin{array}{r} 6\ 3 \\ +\ 3\ 2 \\ \hline \end{array}$$

If it is 95, it means the answer 32 is correct; otherwise, find the subtraction answer again.

⑧

$$\begin{array}{r} 7\ 4 \\ -\ 2\ 9 \\ \hline 5\ 5 \end{array}$$

Check

$$\begin{array}{r} 2\ 9 \\ +\ 5\ 5 \\ \hline \end{array}$$

If it is 74, it means the answer 55 is correct; otherwise, find the subtraction answer again.

⑨

$$\begin{array}{r} 6\ 7 \\ -\ 2\ 8 \\ \hline 3\ 9 \end{array}$$

Check

$$+\ \underline{\qquad}$$

⑩

$$\begin{array}{r} 5\ 2 \\ -\ 1\ 4 \\ \hline 4\ 8 \end{array}$$

Check

$$+\ \underline{\qquad}$$

⑪

$$\begin{array}{r} 7\ 8 \\ -\ 4\ 9 \\ \hline 2\ 7 \end{array}$$

Check

$$+\ \underline{\qquad}$$

⑫

$$\begin{array}{r} 4\ 1 \\ -\ 1\ 6 \\ \hline 3\ 5 \end{array}$$

Check

$$+\ \underline{\qquad}$$

Solve the problems. Then use addition to check the answers.

⑬ Mrs. Green has 75 stamps. If 37 stamps are for girls, how many stamps are for boys?

_____ stamps

⑭ It takes Aunt Amy 61 days to knit a scarf and Aunt Katie 4 days less. How many days does Aunt Katie need to knit a scarf?

_____ days

⑮ Eric has 82 key chains. If he gives 16 key chains to his sister, how many key chains will he have left?

_____ key chains

⑯ Farmer Joe is going to put 96 poles around his field. If 49 poles are put up, how many more will he need to put up?

_____ more

Writing Fact Families:
There are 4 facts in a family. Each fact uses the same 3 numbers.

4 facts:
$$25 + 16 = 41$$
$$16 + 25 = 41$$
$$41 - 25 = 16$$
$$41 - 16 = 25$$

Write the matching family of facts.

⑰
$$17 + 56 \quad = 73$$

_____ + _____ = _____

_____ − _____ = _____

_____ − _____ = _____

⑱
$$90 - 28 \quad = 62$$

_____ + _____ = _____

_____ + _____ = _____

_____ − _____ = _____

Write 4 facts for each family of numbers.

⑲ 43 27 70

_____ = _____

_____ = _____

_____ = _____

_____ = _____

⑳ 14 32 46

_____ = _____

_____ = _____

_____ = _____

_____ = _____

㉑ 15 82 67

_____ = _____

_____ = _____

_____ = _____

_____ = _____

Time and Temperature

- Tell the relationship between days and weeks and between months and years.
- Tell and write time to the quarter-hour.
- Find time intervals.
- Measure temperature with a thermometer.

It took me one hour to finish all the treats.

Read the clues and write the missing information on the calendar. Then fill in the blanks.

①

Judy's Schedule		the month right after June		the year right after 2013		
SUN	**MON**			**THU**		**SAT**
		1	2	3	☀	☀
☀	☀	☀	☀	☀	11	12
13	14			17		
20	21		23			
27		29		31		

☀ Summer Camp

▢ Visiting Grandma

② Judy's summer camp was from _____ to _____ . It lasted ____ days or ____ week.

③ Judy visited her grandma from _____ to _____ . She visited her for ____ days or ____ weeks.

Complete the crossword puzzle with the names of the months.

④

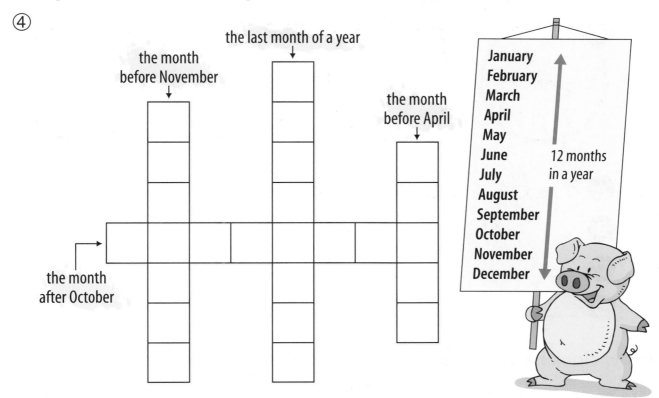

the month before November

the last month of a year

the month before April

the month after October

January
February
March
April
May
June
July
August
September
October
November
December

12 months in a year

Write the ages of the babies in months. Then answer the questions.

⑤

A I am 1 year and 2 months old.

_____ months old

B I am 1 year old.

_____ months old

C I am 1 year and 5 months old.

_____ months old

D I will be 1 year old next month.

_____ months old

⑥ Which baby is the youngest? _____

⑦ Which is the oldest? _____

Tell the times in 2 ways.

⑧

Ⓐ 8 : ____ ; a quarter past ____

Ⓑ ____ : 45 ; a quarter to ____

Ⓒ _____ ; _____

Ⓓ _____ ; _____

Draw clock hands to show the times. Then find the intervals.

⑨ a.

b. It took the girls ____ h to do the dishes.

⑩ a.

a quarter past 2   _a quarter to 3_

b. It took Julia ____ min to finish her dish.

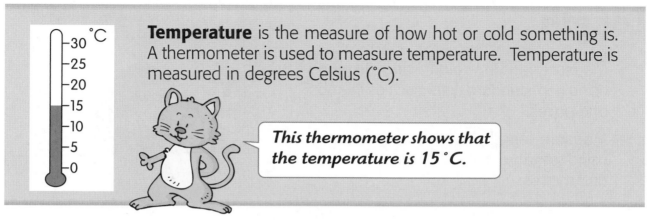

Temperature is the measure of how hot or cold something is. A thermometer is used to measure temperature. Temperature is measured in degrees Celsius (°C).

This thermometer shows that the temperature is 15 °C.

Record the temperatures. Then choose the appropriate clothing to wear. Write the letters.

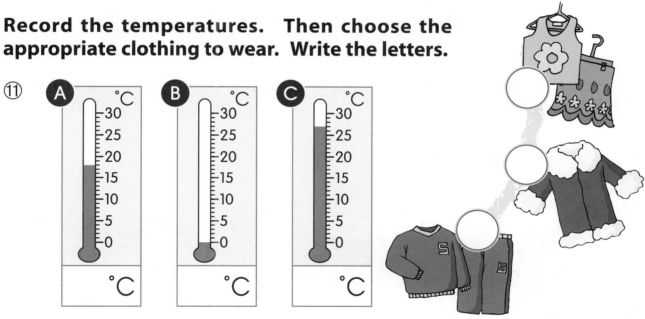

⑪ A °C   B °C   C °C

_____ °C   _____ °C   _____ °C

Colour the thermometer to show the temperature. Then circle the correct answers.

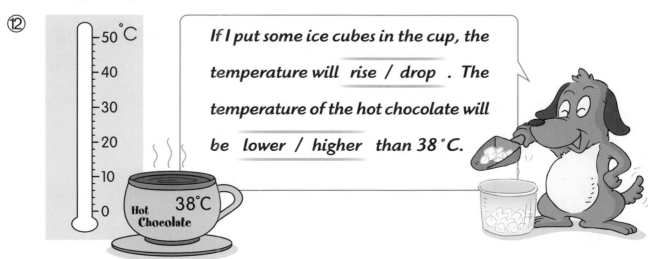

⑫ *If I put some ice cubes in the cup, the temperature will rise / drop . The temperature of the hot chocolate will be lower / higher than 38 °C.*

Hot Chocolate 38°C

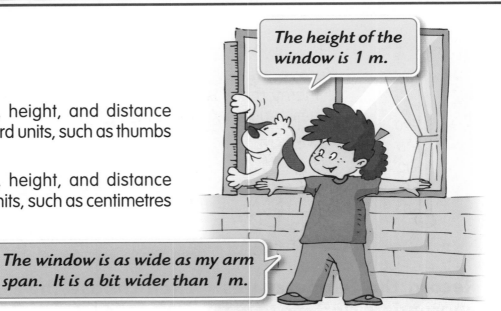

Length

- Measure length, height, and distance using non-standard units, such as thumbs and paces.
- Measure length, height, and distance using standard units, such as centimetres and metres.

The height of the window is 1 m.

The window is as wide as my arm span. It is a bit wider than 1 m.

Use your thumb to measure and record the lengths of the ribbons. Then answer the questions.

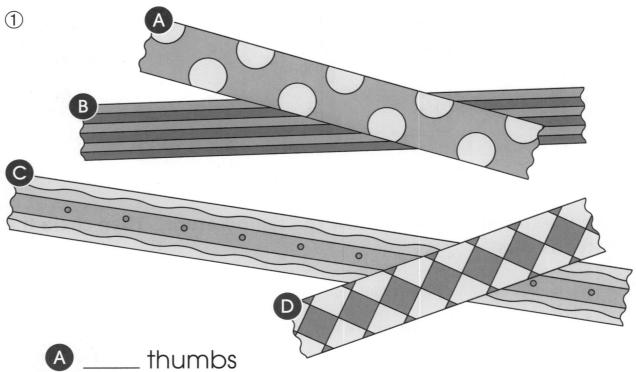

①

A _____ thumbs

B _____ thumbs

C _____ thumbs

D _____ thumbs

② The longest ribbon: _____

③ The shortest ribbon: _____

See how the children do the measurements. Fill in the blanks to complete what they say and circle the correct answers.

④

a. The distance between the sign and the gate is about ＿＿ arm spans or ＿＿ paces.

b. Circle the bigger unit.

⑤

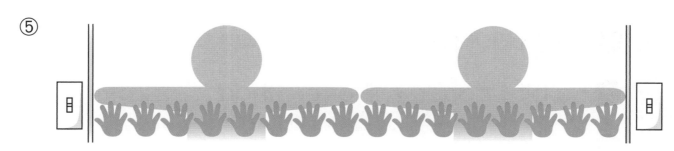

a. The distance between the two switches is ＿＿ arm spans or ＿＿ hand spans.

b. Circle the smaller unit.

Metres (m) and **centimetres (cm)** are units for measuring length.

e.g.

⟵ 2 m ⟶

A bed is about 2 m long.

3 cm

A paper clip is about 3 cm long.

Circle the correct word and write the number to record the length of each worm. Then answer the questions.

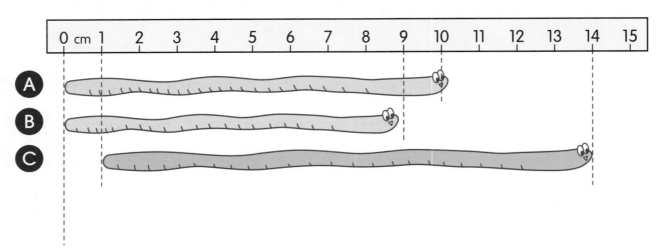

| 0 cm | 1 | 2 | 3 | 4 | 5 | 6 | 7 | 8 | 9 | 10 | 11 | 12 | 13 | 14 | 15 |

Ⓐ

Ⓑ

Ⓒ

⑥ **Ⓐ** : a bit   longer / shorter   than _____

Ⓑ : a bit   longer / shorter   than _____

Ⓒ : _____ long

⑦ Which worm is the longest?   _____

⑧ About how much longer is **Ⓒ** than **Ⓐ** ?   _____

⑨ Draw a worm which is a bit longer than 7 cm below **Ⓒ** .

Trace the dotted lines to complete the grid. Then fill in the blanks and answer the question.

⑩

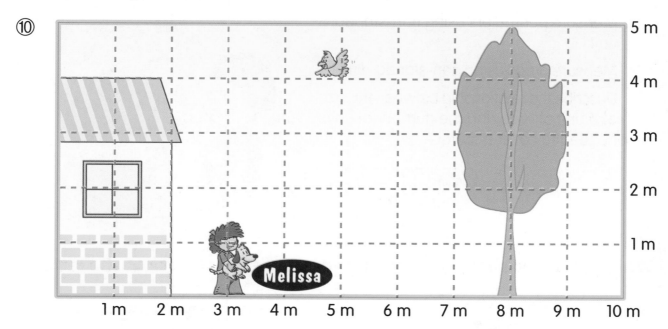

⑪ The house is _____ m high and the tree is _____ m tall.

⑫ Melissa is a bit   taller / shorter   than 1 m.

⑬ The distance between the house and Melissa is _____ .

⑭ Melissa and the tree are _____ apart.

⑮ The bird is flying at _____ above the ground.

⑯ The tree is about _____ wide.

⑰

> *If I walk 2 m toward the tree, what will be the distance between me and the tree?*

_____

Perimeter and Area

- Measure perimeters using non-standard units.
- Measure areas using non-standard units.
- Describe the relationship between the size of a unit of area and the number of units needed to cover a surface.

The area of the hole is about 10 tiles.

Which pictures show the perimeters correctly?   Check ✔ the letters.

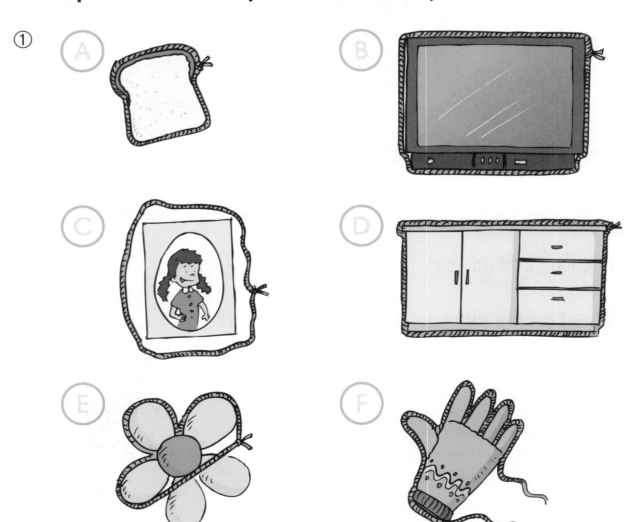

① A

B

C

D

E

F

See how many items are needed to measure the perimeters of the things. Count and record the measurements.

Perimeter

A : about _____ 🖇 long

B : about _____ 🏷 long

C : about _____ 🩹 long

D : about _____ 🍴 long

E : about _____ long

F : about _____ long

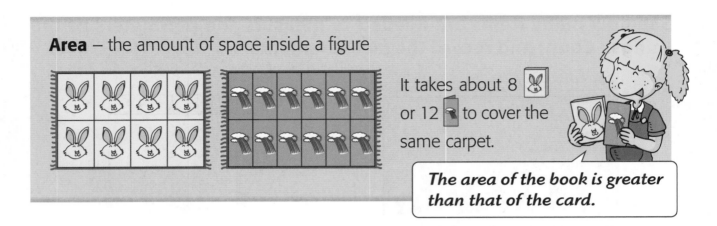

Area – the amount of space inside a figure

It takes about 8 🐰 or 12 📕 to cover the same carpet.

> *The area of the book is greater than that of the card.*

Count and write the number of patches used to cover the same placemat. Then answer the questions.

③

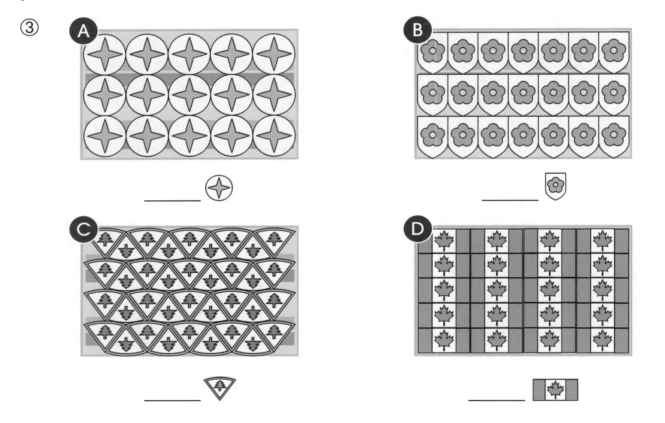

A _____ ✦

B _____

C _____ 🌲

D _____

④ Which patch covers the most space?

⑤ If it takes 18 🍁 to cover a mat, is the area of the mat greater or smaller than that of the placemat? _____

Sometimes we need to combine the parts.

- ▱ and ◹ make ☐ .
- ▯ and ▯ make ☐ .

It takes 8 squares to cover the monster.

Colour each figure. Draw lines to complete the grid. Find the area of each figure. Then answer the questions.

⑥

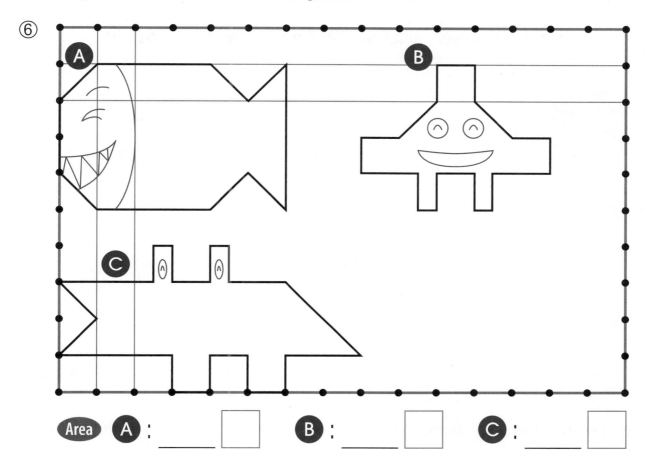

Area   **A** : _____ ☐   **B** : _____ ☐   **C** : _____ ☐

⑦ Which figure has the greatest area?

_____

⑧ *Can you draw a figure with an area of 13 square units in the grid above?*

Money

- Name and state the values of the coins.
- Write money amounts up to 100¢.
- Make a collection of coins equal to $1.

I've found a quarter.

Name the coins. Then write the values.

Dime   Loonie   Nickel   Penny   Quarter   Toonie

①  $ _____

② _____ ¢

③ _____ ¢

④ _____ ¢

⑤  $ _____

⑥ _____ ¢

Check ✔ the correct answers.

⑦ Which coins have a value greater than a dime?

Ⓐ a loonie   Ⓑ a penny   Ⓒ a quarter

⑧ Which coins have a value less than a quarter?

Ⓐ a dime   Ⓑ a penny   Ⓒ a toonie

Find the amount of each group.

⑨

⑩

_____

_____

Draw the fewest coins to show the cost of each toy.

25¢

10¢

5¢

1¢

⑪
48¢

⑫
66¢

⑬
87¢

Draw different coins to show the same value.

 **25¢**  **10¢**  **5¢**  **1¢**

⑭

⑮

Check ✔ the correct number of coins to match each description.

⑯ 5 coins – worth 66¢

⑰ 8 coins – worth 52¢

Cross out ✗ the correct number of coins to make each group worth $1.

⑱

⑲

Read what the children say. Answer their questions. Show your work.

⑳

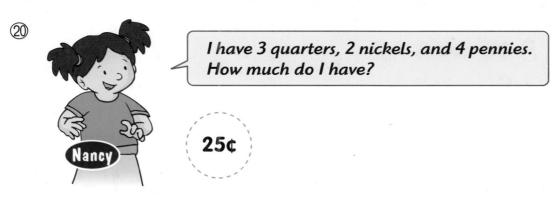

I have 3 quarters, 2 nickels, and 4 pennies. How much do I have?

Nancy

25¢

Nancy has _____ ¢.

㉑

I had 2 quarters, 3 dimes, 2 nickels, and 2 pennies in my purse. Unfortunately, I dropped 1 quarter. How much do I have now?

Katie

Katie has _____ ¢ now.

Addition and Subtraction with Money

- Use addition to find totals.
- Use subtraction to find price differences, sale prices, and change.

Apple Grocery Store	
Bone	37¢
Bone	37¢
Total	74¢
Cash	75¢
Change	1¢

Find the total cost of the items.

 38¢ 19¢ 25¢ 49¢ 27¢

①

$$
\begin{array}{r}
3\,8\ ¢ \\
+\ 2\,7\ ¢ \\
\hline
¢
\end{array}
$$

②

$$+ \underline{}$$

$$\underline{}$$

③

$$+ \underline{}$$

$$\underline{}$$

④

$$+ \underline{}$$

$$\underline{}$$

⑤

$$+ \underline{}$$

$$\underline{}$$

⑥

$$+ \underline{}$$

$$\underline{}$$

⑦

$$+ \underline{}$$

$$\underline{}$$

⑧

$$+ \underline{}$$

$$\underline{}$$

⑨

$$+ \underline{}$$

$$\underline{}$$

Look at the pictures. Find the answers.

⑩

Amount Saved

$$94¢$$
$$-\ 88¢$$
$$\overline{\qquad ¢}$$

⑪

Amount Saved

$$-\ \overline{\qquad}$$
$$\overline{\qquad}$$

⑫

Sale Price

$$55¢$$
$$-\ \ \ 7¢$$
$$\overline{\qquad ¢}$$

⑬

Sale Price

$$-\ \overline{\qquad}$$
$$\overline{\qquad}$$

⑭ *Each item costs 46¢ now.*

Item	Regular Price	Money Saved
a key chain	70¢	
a doll	67¢	
a bookmark	95¢	
a puzzle	82¢	

⑮

Each figurine saves

28¢.

Figurine	Regular Price	Sale Price
A	95¢	
B	44¢	
C	60¢	
D	53¢	

Write how much each child has. Then solve the problems.

⑯

a. Tom has _____ ¢ .

b. If Tom buys [18¢], how much will he have left?

_____

_____

⑰

a. Tina has _____ ¢ .

b. If Tina buys JUICE [46¢], how much will she have left?

_____

_____

⑱

I have 2 dimes and 4 pennies. — Sue

I have 2 quarters and 1 nickel. — Ted

a. Sue has _____ ¢ and Ted has _____ ¢.

b. How much do the children have in all?

_____

_____

Look at the Christmas ornaments. Help the children solve the problems. Show your work. Circle the correct answers.

⑲ _Here is my change from 75¢. Which ornament did I buy?_

_____ = _____

⑳ _I want to buy ⊙ and ⊙. If I pay with 4 quarters, what is my change?_

_____ = _____

㉑ _I paid 3 quarters and 1 nickel for 2 ornaments, but I broke them by accident. Which 2 did I buy?_

_____ = _____

2-D Shapes (1)

- Identify and describe different shapes.
- Sort 2-D shapes by the number of sides and vertices.
- Use different shapes to design patterns.

Join the dots in order to complete each shape. Then name it.

triangle   square   rectangle   pentagon   hexagon   heptagon   octagon

①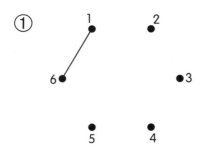

_____

②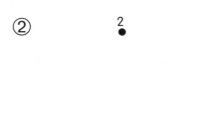

_____

③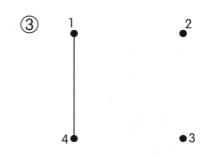

_____

④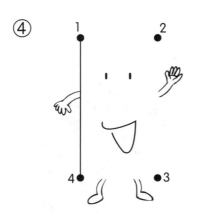

_____

⑤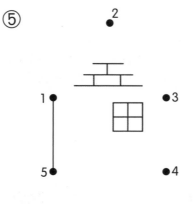

_____

⑥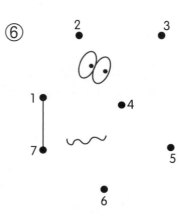

_____

Trace the sides and circle the vertices of each shape with a red coloured pencil. Then answer the questions.

⑦ **A** 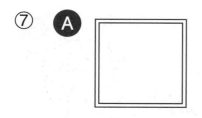 **B**  **C**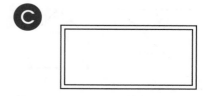

D 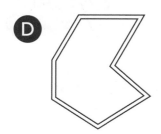 **E** 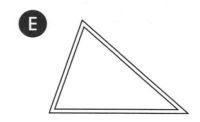 **F**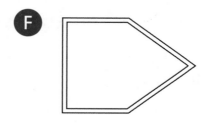

G  **H** 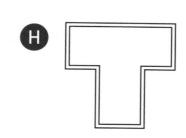 **I**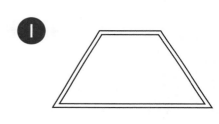

⑧ a. Which shape has 5 sides?   _____

   b. Does the shape also have 5 vertices?   _____

⑨ a. Which shapes have 4 vertices?   _____

   b. How many sides does each shape have?   ____ sides

⑩ Draw a hexagon which is different from the one above.

See what shapes Judy drew. Help her sort the shapes. Draw them in the correct grids.

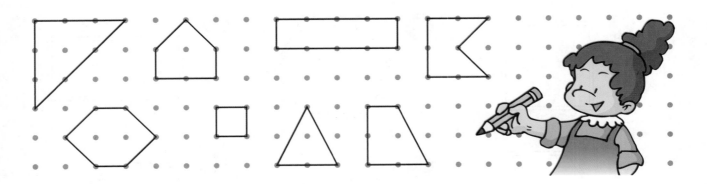

⑪ with 5 vertices

⑫ with 4 or fewer vertices

⑬ with 4 sides

⑭ with 5 or more sides

Name the shapes used in each pattern. Then use the same group of shapes to create a pattern different from the one given.

⑮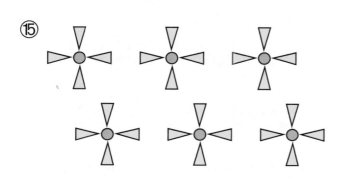

_____

⑯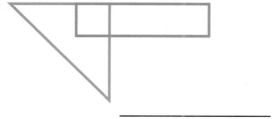

_____

Colour and name the overlapping part of each pair of shapes.

⑰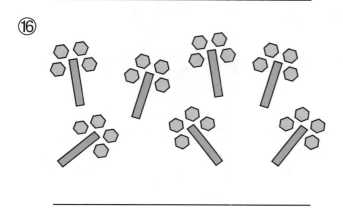

_____

⑱

⑲

_____   _____

2-D Shapes (2)

- Identify and describe regular shapes.
- Build different things using tangrams.
- Describe the locations and the movements of objects.

We're two steps apart.

Read what Simon says. Then help him colour the correct shapes.

A regular shape has all sides equal.

① **a regular pentagon**

   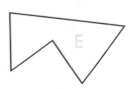

A　　B　　C　　D　　E

② **a regular hexagon**

   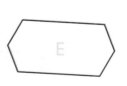

A　　B　　C　　D　　E

③ **a regular octagon**

 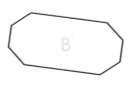  

A　　B　　C　　D　　E

Name the shape of each piece in a tangram. Then answer the questions.

triangle △   square ▢   parallelogram ▱

④

Piece	Shape
A	
B	
C	
D	
E	
F	
G	

⑤ Colour A and the one which is the same as A yellow.

⑥ Colour C and the one which is the same as C red.

Trace the dotted lines to complete the things built by a tangram. Then name the things.

⑦

⑧

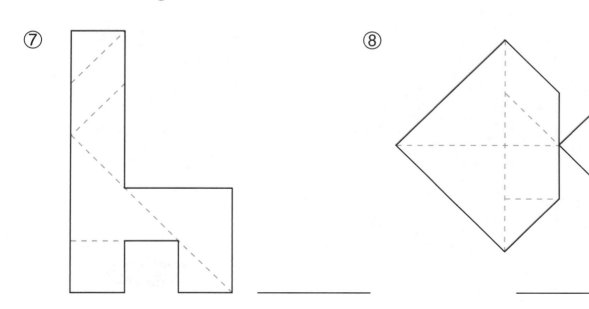

Check ✔ the pictures that are made by a tangram. Then write the number of pieces used and name the pictures.

⑨ Ⓐ

◯ ; _____

Ⓑ

◯ ; _____

Ⓒ

◯ ; _____

Ⓓ

◯ ; _____

Ⓔ

◯ ; _____

Ⓕ

◯ ; _____

Read what Mrs. Smith says. Draw the children's new positions.

⑩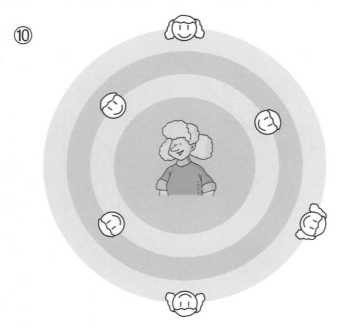

Boys take 1 step back.
Girls take 2 steps forward.

Mrs. Smith

Words for describing   e.g.

- the relative locations of objects:
  beside, to the right/left of
- the movement of objects:
  walk around/down, crawl under, go to

The path shows that Tommy walked around the desk, down the aisle, and over to the window.

Read the sentences. Draw the objects and the path.

- A ball is beside the box and a cup is in front of the box.
- Two apples are under the bridge.
- A dog is sitting two steps to the left of the chair.
- A treasure box is on the carpet.

⑪

Tom walks over the bridge and around the box. Then he walks around the chair and goes over to the treasure box.

Symmetry

- Identify symmetrical pictures.
- Draw the line(s) of symmetry in a picture or shape.
- Draw the missing part of a symmetrical picture.
- Describe symmetrical designs.

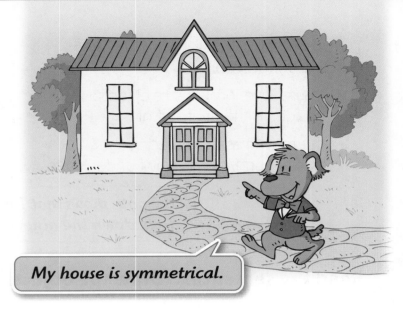

My house is symmetrical.

Colour the symmetrical pictures.

①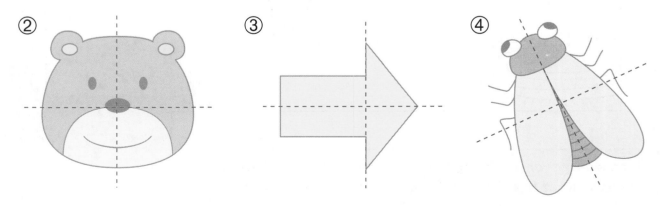

Which dotted line is the line of symmetry of each picture? Trace it.

② ③ ④

Draw the line of symmetry of each picture.

⑤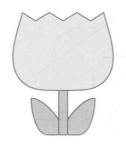

⑥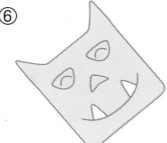

⑦

⑧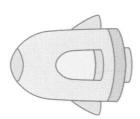

⑨

⑩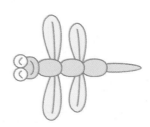

The dotted lines are the lines of symmetry. Trace them. Then count and write the correct numbers.

⑪

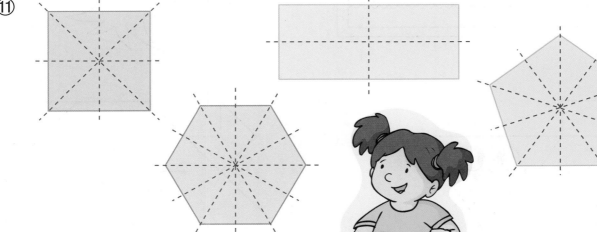

There are _____ lines of symmetry in a square, _____ in a rectangle, _____ in a regular pentagon, and _____ in a regular hexagon.

Draw the missing parts of each symmetrical picture.

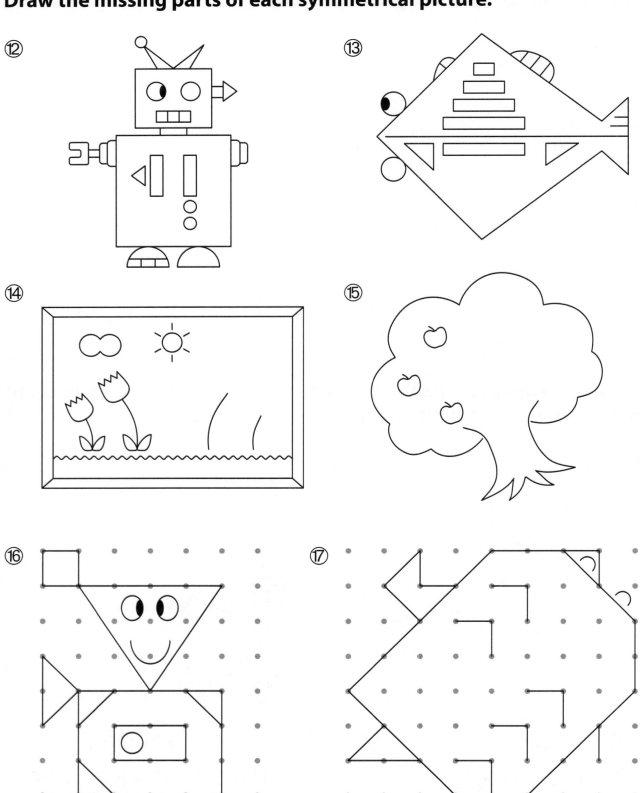

Ways to describe symmetrical designs:

I've made a symmetrical design that looks like a butterfly.

I've used 3 rectangles and 2 triangles to make a symmetrical design.

Describe each symmetrical design.

⑱ _____

_____

⑲ _____

_____

⑳ _____

_____

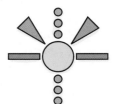

Read what Robin the Dog says. Colour the correct picture.

㉑ I've made a symmetrical design that looks like my favourite snack.

      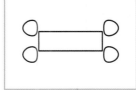

3-D Figures

- Identify 3-D figures.
- Sort and classify 3-D figures by their properties.
- Describe the skeletons of prisms and pyramids.

Colour the prisms red and the pyramids yellow.

①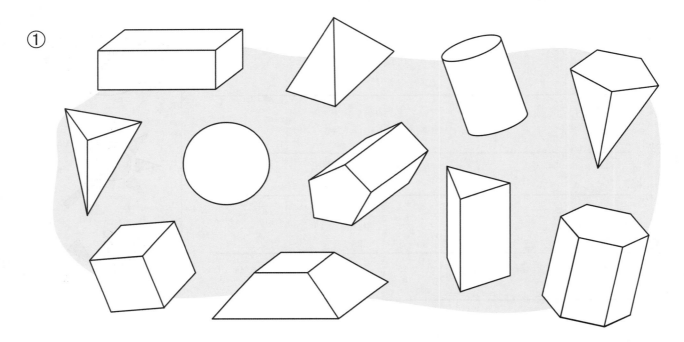

Name the 3-D figures.

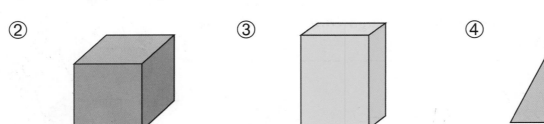

② _____

③ _____

④ _____

Trace the dotted lines and write which two 3-D figures you can see in each model.

cone   cube   cylinder   prism   pyramid   sphere

⑤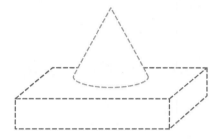

_____   _____

⑥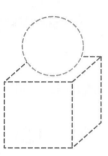

_____   _____

⑦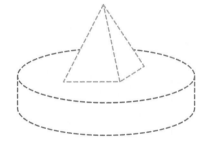

_____   _____

⑧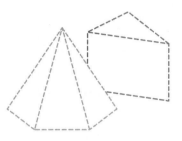

_____   _____

Name the coloured faces.

⑨

_____

⑩

_____

⑪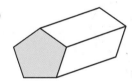

_____

⑫

_____

⑬

_____

⑭

_____

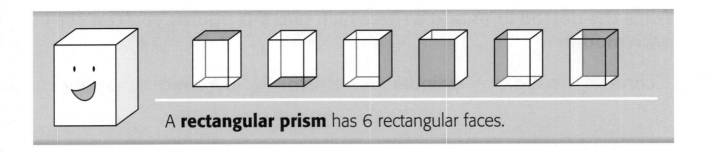

A **rectangular prism** has 6 rectangular faces.

Sort the 3-D figures. Write the letters. Then complete the descriptions.

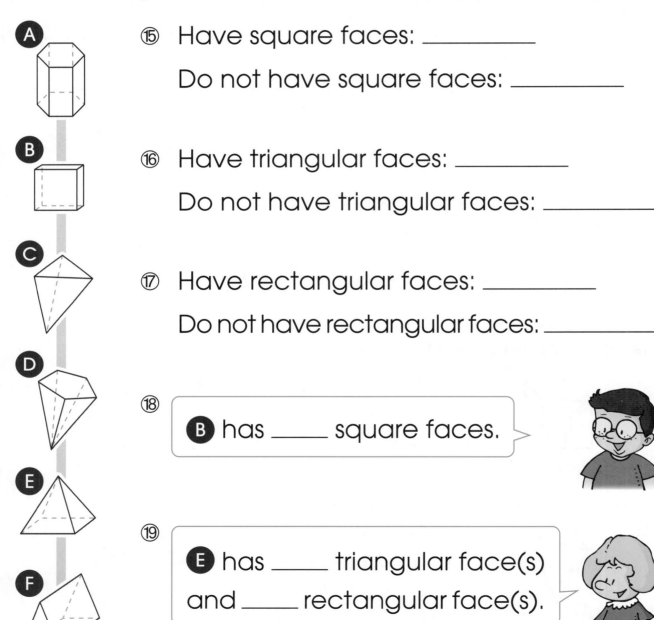

⑮ Have square faces: _____

Do not have square faces: _____

⑯ Have triangular faces: _____

Do not have triangular faces: _____

⑰ Have rectangular faces: _____

Do not have rectangular faces: _____

⑱ **B** has ____ square faces.

⑲ **E** has ____ triangular face(s) and ____ rectangular face(s).

You can use straws and strings, sticks and marshmallows, or sticks and modelling clay to make skeletons of prisms and pyramids.

e.g.

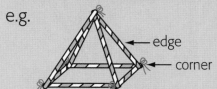

← edge

← corner

This pyramid has 8 edges and 5 corners.

Look at the skeleton of each 3-D figure. Count and write the numbers of edges and corners that each figure has.

⑳

____ edges

____ corners

㉑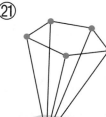

____ edges

____ corners

㉒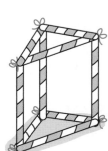

____ edges

____ corners

㉓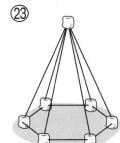

____ edges

____ corners

Answer Bob's questions.

㉔

If I fold up the triangle, what 3–D figure will I get? How many sticks and marshmallows do I need to build the same figure?

He will get a _____ . He needs

____ sticks and ____ marshmallows.

Multiplication (1)

- Understand multiplication as repeated addition.
- Read and write multiplication sentences.
- Multiply by 2, 3, 4, 5, and 10.

> 5 groups of 2 are 10.

5 times 2
= 5 x 2
= 10

Circle the objects. Then fill in the blanks.

① Circle every 2 apples.

$2 + 2 + 2 + 2 + 2 +$ _____

$= 6$ groups of _____

$=$ _____ times 2

$=$ _____

② Circle every 4 stars.

$4 + 4 + 4 + 4 +$ _____

$=$ _____ groups of 4

$= 5$ times _____

$=$ _____

③ Circle every 3 bells.

$3 + 3 + 3 + 3 +$ _____

$=$ _____ groups of 3

$=$ _____ times 3

$=$ _____

Look at the pictures. Fill in the blanks.

④ $5 + 5 + 5 + 5 +$ ___ $+$ ___

     $= 6$ groups of ___

     $= 6 \times$ ___

     $=$ ___

⑤ $3 + 3 + 3 + 3 +$ ___ $+$ ___ $+$ ___ $+$ ___

     $=$ ___ groups of ___

     $=$ ___ $\times$ ___

     $=$ ___

⑥ $4 + 4 + 4 +$ ___ $+$ ___ $+$ ___ $+$ ___

     $=$ ___ groups of ___

     $=$ ___ $\times$ ___

     $=$ ___

Draw the correct number of pictures to match each multiplication sentence.

⑦ $4 \times 3 = 12$

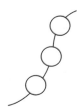

⑧ $3 \times 5 = 15$

Draw the arrows to continue the patterns. Then count by 2's, 5's, or 10's to write the missing numbers.

⑨

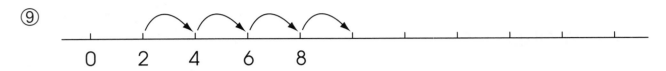

0   2   4   6   8

⑩

0   5   10   15   20

⑪

0   10   20   30   40

Complete the multiplication tables with the help of the number lines above.

⑫ 1 x 2 = _____

2 x 2 = _____

3 x 2 = _____

4 x 2 = _____

5 x 2 = _____

6 x 2 = _____

7 x 2 = _____

8 x 2 = _____

9 x 2 = _____

10 x 2 = _____

⑬ 1 x 5 = _____

2 x 5 = _____

3 x 5 = _____

4 x 5 = _____

5 x 5 = _____

6 x 5 = _____

7 x 5 = _____

8 x 5 = _____

9 x 5 = _____

10 x 5 = _____

⑭ 1 x 10 = _____

2 x 10 = _____

3 x 10 = _____

4 x 10 = _____

5 x 10 = _____

6 x 10 = _____

7 x 10 = _____

8 x 10 = _____

9 x 10 = _____

10 x 10 = _____

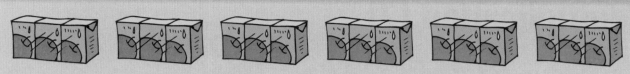

6 groups of 3
= 6 x 3
= **18**   There are 18 boxes of juice.

Look at the pictures. Find the answers.

⑮
Look at the eyes of the aliens.

a. 2 x 3 = _____   b. 9 x 3 = _____

c. 7 x 3 = _____   d. 5 x 3 = _____

e. 4 x 3 = _____   f. 3 x 3 = _____

⑯ *Look at the legs of the aliens.*

a. 6 x 4 = _____   b. 5 x 4 = _____

c. 7 x 4 = _____   d. 9 x 4 = _____

e. 3 x 4 = _____   f. 4 x 4 = _____

Read what Lucy says. Draw the rings and answer the question.

⑰ *There are 4 rings on each stick. How many rings do I have in all?*

_____ rings

Multiplication (2)

- Multiply a 1-digit number by 6, 7, 8, or 9.
- Complete multiplication tables.
- Solve problems involving multiplication.

There are 18 eyes staring at me.

Look at the pictures. Do the multiplication.

①

1 x 6 = _____

2 x 6 = _____

3 x 6 = _____

4 x 6 = _____

5 x 6 = _____

6 x 6 = _____

7 x 6 = _____

8 x 6 = _____

9 x 6 = _____

10 x 6 = _____

②

1 x 7 = _____

2 x 7 = _____

3 x 7 = _____

4 x 7 = _____

5 x 7 = _____

6 x 7 = _____

7 x 7 = _____

8 x 7 = _____

9 x 7 = _____

10 x 7 = _____

Do the multiplication with the help of the pictures. Then answer the questions.

③

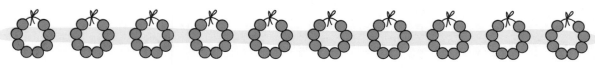

a.
$$\begin{array}{r} 8 \\ \times\quad 4 \\ \hline \end{array}$$

b.
$$\begin{array}{r} 8 \\ \times\quad 2 \\ \hline \end{array}$$

c.
$$\begin{array}{r} 8 \\ \times\quad 8 \\ \hline \end{array}$$

d. 7 x 8 = _____

e. 3 x 8 = _____

f. 6 x 8 = _____

g. 9 x 8 = _____

④ | *How many beads are there in 10 bracelets?*

_____ = _____   _____ beads

⑤

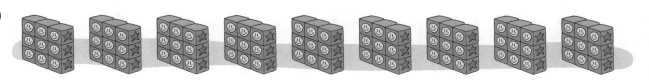

a.
$$\begin{array}{r} 9 \\ \times\quad 5 \\ \hline \end{array}$$

b.
$$\begin{array}{r} 9 \\ \times\quad 2 \\ \hline \end{array}$$

c.
$$\begin{array}{r} 9 \\ \times\quad 7 \\ \hline \end{array}$$

d. 6 x 9 = _____

e. 9 x 9 = _____

f. 8 x 9 = _____

g. 1 x 9 = _____

⑥ | *How many blocks are needed to build 4 stacks?*

_____ = _____   _____ blocks

Do the multiplication.

⑦
$$\begin{array}{r} 7 \\ \times\ \ 4 \\ \hline \end{array}$$

⑧
$$\begin{array}{r} 6 \\ \times\ \ 3 \\ \hline \end{array}$$

⑨
$$\begin{array}{r} 8 \\ \times\ \ 10 \\ \hline \end{array}$$

⑩
$$\begin{array}{r} 9 \\ \times\ \ 4 \\ \hline \end{array}$$

⑪ 8 x 6 = _____

⑫ 3 x 9 = _____

⑬ 2 x 7 = _____

⑭ 4 x 8 = _____

⑮ 7 x 9 = _____

⑯ 6 x 7 = _____

⑰ 3 x 8 = _____

⑱ 9 x 6 = _____

The answer of each question is the number of candies in each box. Find the answer. Then answer the questions.

⑲
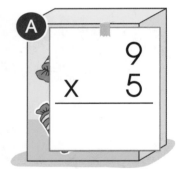

A
$$\begin{array}{r} 9 \\ \times\ \ 5 \\ \hline \end{array}$$

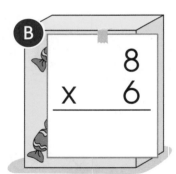

B
$$\begin{array}{r} 8 \\ \times\ \ 6 \\ \hline \end{array}$$

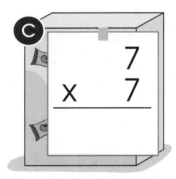

C
$$\begin{array}{r} 7 \\ \times\ \ 7 \\ \hline \end{array}$$

D   3 x 6 = ____

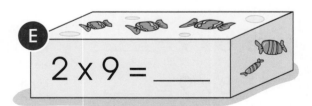

E   2 x 9 = ____

⑳ Which box has the most candies?   ____

㉑ Which box has 1 fewer candy than ?   ____

Solve the problems.

㉒ Each jar has 9 gumballs. How many gumballs are there in 6 jars?

_____ gumballs

㉓ Katie has 7 boxes of chocolates. How many chocolates does she have in all?

_____ chocolates

㉔ There are 8 groups of 6 girls. How many girls are there in all?

_____ girls

㉕ How many days are there in 4 weeks?

_____ days

㉖ *If I play with 6 aliens, how many eyes will I see?*

_____ eyes

More about Multiplication

We have the same number of fish.

- Multiply by 0 and 1.
- Solve problems involving multiplication.
- Understand interesting multiplication.

3 x 2   =   2 x 3

Look at the pictures. Complete the number sentences and find the answers.

①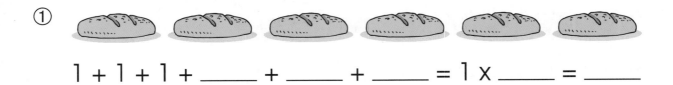

1 + 1 + 1 + _____ + _____ + _____ = 1 x _____ = _____

②

0 + 0 + 0 + _____ + _____ = 0 x _____ = _____

③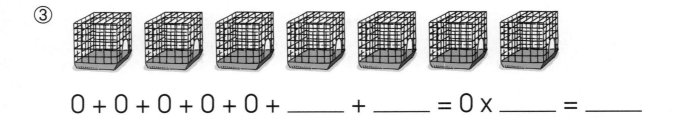

0 + 0 + 0 + 0 + 0 + _____ + _____ = 0 x _____ = _____

④

1 + 1 + _____ + _____ = 1 x _____ = _____

Find the answers.

⑤
$$\begin{array}{r} 3 \\ \times\ 4 \\ \hline \end{array}$$

⑥
$$\begin{array}{r} 0 \\ \times\ 8 \\ \hline \end{array}$$

⑦
$$\begin{array}{r} 1 \\ \times\ 9 \\ \hline \end{array}$$

⑧
$$\begin{array}{r} 2 \\ \times\ 6 \\ \hline \end{array}$$

⑨
$$\begin{array}{r} 0 \\ \times\ 5 \\ \hline \end{array}$$

⑩
$$\begin{array}{r} 7 \\ \times\ 3 \\ \hline \end{array}$$

⑪
$$\begin{array}{r} 1 \\ \times\ 2 \\ \hline \end{array}$$

⑫
$$\begin{array}{r} 4 \\ \times\ 8 \\ \hline \end{array}$$

⑬ $2 \times 5 =$ _____

⑭ $3 \times 6 =$ _____

⑮ $7 \times 7 =$ _____

⑯ $5 \times 4 =$ _____

⑰ $9 \times 0 =$ _____

⑱ $3 \times 1 =$ _____

⑲ *Each snowman has 1 carrot. How many carrots do 6 snowmen have in all?*

_____ carrots

⑳ Each snowman has 2 sticks. How many sticks do 7 snowmen have in all?

_____ sticks

㉑ The snowmen have no legs. How many legs do 4 snowmen have in all?

_____ legs

Even if the order of multiplication changes, the product is still the same.

e.g.

3 x 4   =   4 x 3

=

Each group has 12 bananas.

Look at the pictures. Draw the missing items. Then fill in the blanks.

㉒

2 x 6 = 6 x ____

Each group has ____ beads.

㉓

3 x 5 = ____ x 3

Each group has ____ flowers.

㉔

4 x 7 = 7 x ____

Each group has ____ stickers.

Complete the multiplication sentences.

㉕ 6 x 4 = 4 x _____

       = _____

㉖ 3 x 7 = _____ x 3

       = _____

㉗ 5 x 8 = 8 x _____

       = _____

㉘ 4 x 9 = _____ x 4

       = _____

The animals in each group have the same number of treats. Help them draw the rest of the pictures and fill in the blanks.

㉙

I have 2 groups of 6 carrots.

I have 6 groups of _____ carrots.

㉚

I have 3 groups of 5 bones.

I have 5 groups of _____ bones.

Division

- Divide a set of objects into equal groups.
- Divide a set of objects into equal shares.
- Understand the relationship between multiplication and division.

Colour the items in each group with the same colour. Then fill in the blanks.

2 dogs share 16 bones.
Each dog has 8 bones.

① Put 4 planes in a group.

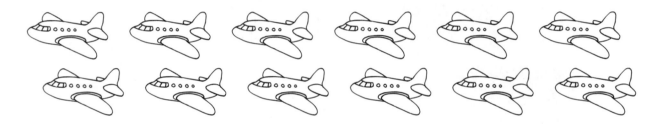

There are _____ planes. If there are 4 planes in a group, there will be _____ groups in all.

② Put 5 bells in a group.

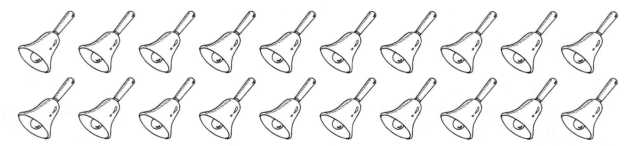

There are _____ bells. If there are 5 bells in a group, there will be _____ groups in all.

Trace the dotted lines to put the items into groups. Follow the pattern to put the rest of the items. Then fill in the blanks.

③ Put 12 fish equally into 3 fishbowls.

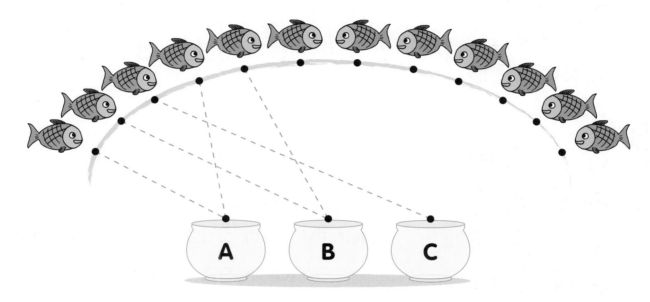

Each fishbowl holds _____ fish.

④ 5 girls share 15 flowers equally.

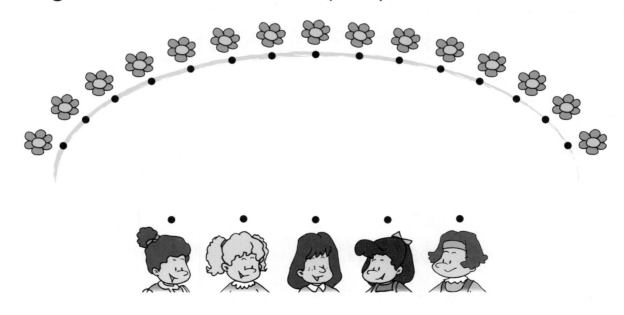

Each girl gets _____ flowers.

Fill in the blanks with the help of the given pictures.

⑤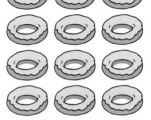

   a. There are _____ doughnuts.

   b. If the doughnuts are put in bags of 3, there are _____ bags in all.

⑥

   a. There are _____ ornaments.

   b. If Mr. Shaw puts all the ornaments equally into 5 bags, there are _____ ornaments in each bag.

Draw 24 fish in the sea. Then fill in the blanks.

⑦ a.

   b. If the fish are divided into groups of 4, there are _____ groups in all.

   c. If Mr. Shark divides the fish equally into 8 groups, there are _____ fish in each group.

Division is the opposite of multiplication.

e.g.

2 rows of **3** apples
= **2** three's
= **2** x **3**
= **6**

Put 6 apples into 2 groups. There are 3 apples in each group.

Draw the pictures to match the multiplication sentence. Then fill in the blanks.

⑧   3 rows of 7 sticks

= 3 x _____

= _____

  Put _____ equally into 7 groups. There are _____ in each group.

⑨   4 rows of 6 marbles

= 4 x _____

= _____

  Put _____ equally into 6 groups. There are _____ in each group.

Read what Mary says. Solve the problem.

⑩   *If I put 35 bones equally into 7 bowls, how many bones are there in each bowl?*

_____ bones

Fractions (1)

- Use fractional names, such as halves, thirds, and fourths, to describe the equal parts of a whole object or a set of objects.
- Understand the relationship between the number of fractional parts of a whole and the size of the fractional parts.

We each have 1 part of a pizza.

But my part is smaller because my pizza is cut into more parts.

Colour one half of each figure.

①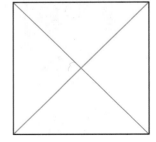

②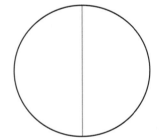

③

Colour two thirds of each figure.

④

⑤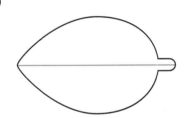

⑥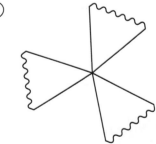

Colour three fourths of each figure.

⑦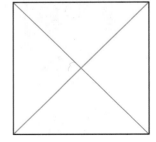

⑧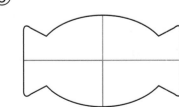

⑨

Check ✔ the correct figures.

⑩ Two sixths is coloured.

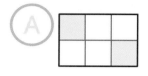 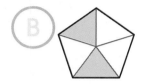 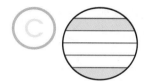 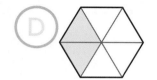

⑪ Three eighths is coloured.

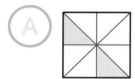 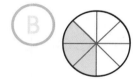 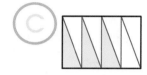 

⑫ Two fifths is coloured.

  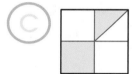 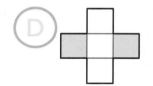

Write a fraction for the coloured part(s) in each figure.

⑬

_____ sixths

⑭

_____

⑮

_____

⑯

_____

⑰

_____

⑱
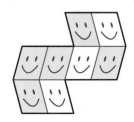

_____

Trace the dotted lines to divide the items in each group into equal parts. Then colour the parts and fill in the blanks with fractional names.

⑲ a.

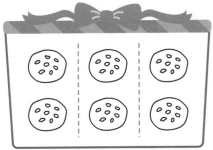

b. Colour two parts.

c. _____ of the 🍪 are coloured.

⑳ a.

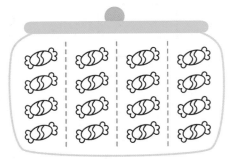

b. Colour three parts.

c. _____ of the 🍬 are coloured.

Put the items into equal groups. Then fill in the blanks.

㉑ Put the flowers into 3 equal groups and colour 2 groups red.

❀ ❀ ❀ ❀ ❀ ❀

❀ ❀ ❀ ❀ ❀ ❀   _____ are red.

㉒ Put the cars into 6 equal groups and colour 5 groups blue.

🚌 🚌 🚌 🚌 🚌 🚌

🚌 🚌 🚌 🚌 🚌 🚌   _____ are blue.

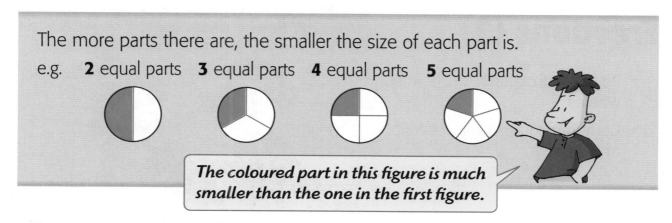

The more parts there are, the smaller the size of each part is.

e.g.   **2** equal parts   **3** equal parts   **4** equal parts   **5** equal parts

The coloured part in this figure is much smaller than the one in the first figure.

See how the paper is folded. Use fractions to describe the parts that you see. Then draw the folds back on the paper and write the number of equal parts.

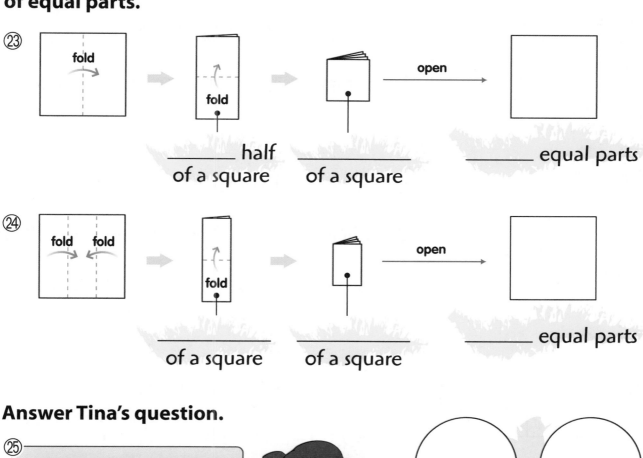

㉓   fold

fold   open

_____ **half**
of a square   _____
of a square   _____ **equal parts**

㉔   fold   fold

fold   open

_____
of a square   _____
of a square   _____ **equal parts**

Answer Tina's question.

㉕

Which is bigger, one third of a pizza or two fourths of a pizza? Use the circles to prove your answer.

_____

Fractions (2)

- Regroup fractional parts into wholes.
- Compare fractions with the help of diagrams.

> **Don't worry. 2 halves make 1. You still have a whole cake.**

> **Mom, Dave has cut my cake.**

Trace the dotted lines. Then fill in the blanks.

①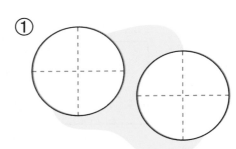

a. _____ fourths form a whole.

b. Eight _____ form two wholes.

②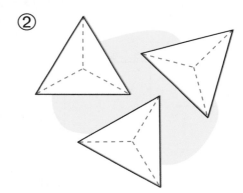

a. _____ thirds form a whole.

b. Nine _____ form three wholes.

c. Six thirds form _____ wholes.

③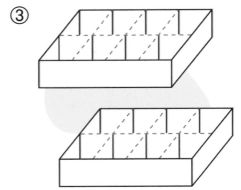

a. _____ eighths form a whole.

b. Sixteen eighths form _____ wholes.

c. _____ eighths form half of a whole.

Complete the diagrams to illustrate what the children say.

④ *Combine nine fourths to form two wholes and one fourth.*

⑤ *Combine seven halves to form three wholes and one half.*

⑥ *Combine five thirds to form one whole and two thirds.*

Write a sentence to describe each group of diagrams.

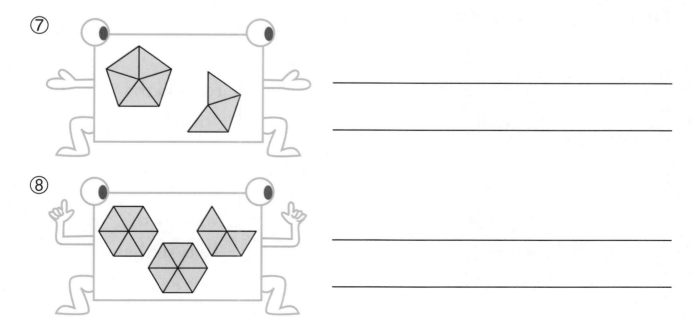

⑦

⑧

Colour the correct number of parts to match the fractions. Then fill in the blanks with "greater" or "smaller".

⑨　a.　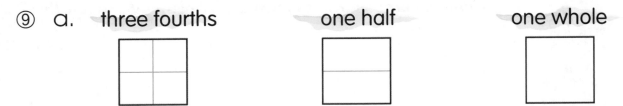

three fourths　　　　one half　　　　one whole

b.　Three fourths is _____ than one half.

c.　Three fourths is _____ than one whole.

⑩　a.　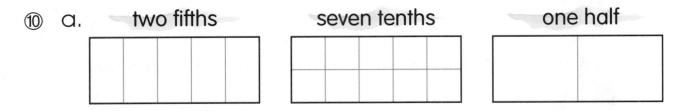

two fifths　　　　seven tenths　　　　one half

b.　Two fifths is _____ than seven tenths.

c.　One half is _____ than seven tenths.

Circle the greater fraction in each pair.

⑪

three eighths

one half

⑫

four sixths

one half

⑬

two thirds

three tenths

⑭

one fifth

two sixths

Draw lines and colour the correct number of parts of the diagrams to match the fractions. Then fill in the blanks.

⑮　a.　　three fifths　　　　two fourths　　　　one third

b.

_____ is the greatest; _____

is the smallest.

⑯　a.　　two tenths　　　　three fourths　　　　one half

b.

_____ is greater than _____ ,

but smaller than _____ .

Read what Dave says. Answer his question.

⑰

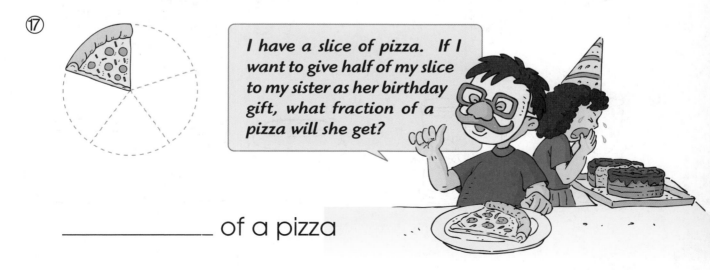

> I have a slice of pizza. If I want to give half of my slice to my sister as her birthday gift, what fraction of a pizza will she get?

_____ of a pizza

Capacity

- Compare and order a collection of containers by capacity.
- Measure and record the capacities of containers using non-standard units.

What I guessed is correct. This flower pot can hold 6 cans of pop.

Colour the container with the greatest capacity.

①

②

③

④

⑤

⑥

Put the containers in order from the one with the greatest capacity to the one with the least.

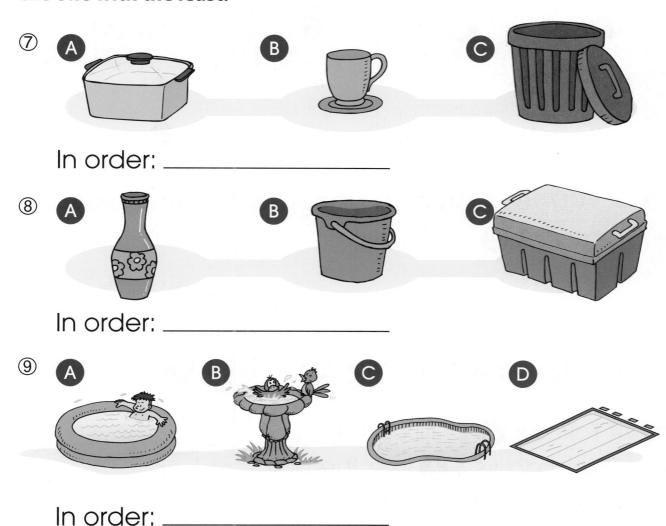

⑦ A   B   C

In order: _____

⑧ A   B   C

In order: _____

⑨ A   B   C   D

In order: _____

Draw two containers, one with a greater capacity and one with a smaller capacity than the one shown.

⑩   ⑪

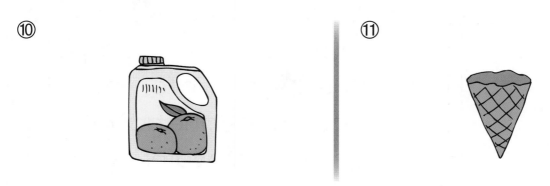

Estimate the capacities of the containers.   Then circle the answers.

⑫   B / C   can hold more water than Ⓐ.

⑬   A / B   can hold about the same amount of water as Ⓓ.

⑭   C / D   has the greatest capacity.

⑮   It takes about 4 / 40 Ⓑ to fill up Ⓐ.

⑯   It takes 5 Ⓐ to fill up a pail. If David pours 3 Ⓐ into the pail, colour the pail to show how much water it holds.

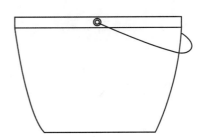

⑰   Tommy has poured 2 Ⓐ of water into his aquarium. If he pours 2 more Ⓐ of water into the aquarium, colour the aquarium to show how much water it will hold.

Help each child choose the most appropriate thing to do the measurement. Circle the correct answer.

⑱  *If I want to measure the capacity of the bowl of my dog, which would be the best unit?*

a spoon   a milk jug   a garbage can

⑲ *I want to measure the capacity of my bathtub. Which would be the best unit?*

a lunch box   a perfume bottle   a pail

⑳ *I want to measure the capacity of my water bottle. Which would be the best unit?*

a dropper   a cup   a pot

What will you use to measure the capacity of the containers below? Give your suggestions on the lines.

㉑

_____

㉒

_____

㉓

㉔ *I like this cookie jar.*

_____

Mass

- Compare the masses of objects.
- Estimate, measure, and record the masses of objects using non-standard units.

> *I can lift up the heaviest one.*

Colour the heaviest one in each group.

①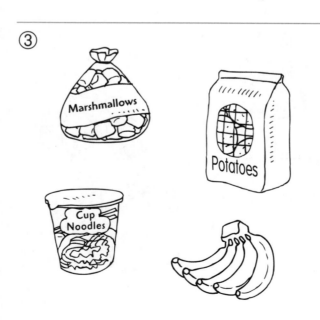

②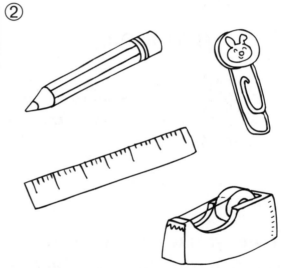

③

④

Look at the pictures. Answer the questions and fill in the blanks.

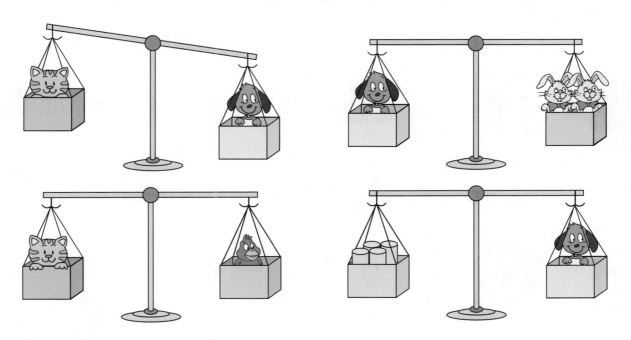

⑤ Which animal is heavier, the cat or the dog? _____

⑥ Which animal is heavier, the dog or the rabbit? _____

⑦ Which animal has the same weight as the cat? _____

⑧ Which animal is the heaviest? _____

⑨ The dog has the same weight as _____ cylinders.

⑩ The rabbits have the same weight as _____ cylinders. Each rabbit weighs about the same as _____ cylinders.

Look at the pictures. Record the weight of each thing. Then answer the questions.

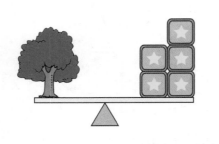

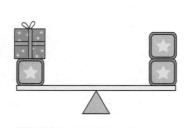

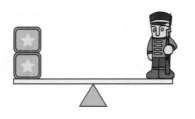

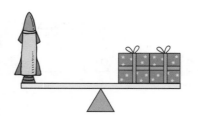

⑪ **Weight**

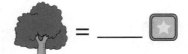 = ____ ⭐   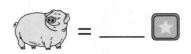 = ____ ⭐

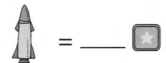 = ____ ⭐   = ____ ⭐

 = ____ ⭐

⑫

Colour the heaviest thing yellow. Then colour the things that have the same weight blue.

⑬ The pig has the same weight as 1 tree and ____ nutcracker(s).

⑭ The tree has the same weight as 1 gift box and ____ rocket(s).

Read what the children say. Help them circle the best units to do the measurements.

⑮

 *I want to know the weight of my cat. Which thing should I use?*

⑯

I want to know the weight of my apple. Which thing should I use?

⑰

Which thing should I use to measure the weight of my mom's fully-packed suitcase?

Read what Sam says. Help him draw the correct number of bricks to balance himself.

⑱

I have the same weight as 12 bricks.

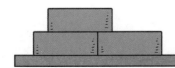

Patterns (1)

He can make a pattern with his whip.

- Identify, describe, extend, and create repeating, growing, and shrinking patterns.
- Understand the concept of equality between pairs of expressions.

Put a check mark ✔ in the circle if there is a pattern in each group and draw the one that comes next; otherwise, put a cross ✘ in the circle.

Next

①

② 3 5 2 2 1 9 3 8

③

④ 90 80 70 60 50 40 30

⑤

Follow each pattern to draw the next two pictures. Then write "shrinking" or "growing".

⑥

It is a _____ pattern.

⑦ 45 50 55 60 65 70 75

It is a _____ pattern.

⑧ AAAAAAA   AAAAAA   AAAAA   AAAA

It is a _____ pattern.

⑨

a _____ pattern

Use the pictures in each pattern to create a different pattern from the one given.

⑩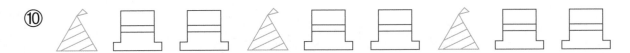

_____

⑪

_____

⑫

_____

Follow the pattern to write the next two number sentences.   Then write "growing" or "shrinking".

⑬ 13 + 1 = 14
   13 + 2 = 15
   13 + 3 = 16
   13 + 4 = 17

⑭ 70 – 1 = 69
   70 – 2 = 68
   70 – 3 = 67
   70 – 4 = 66

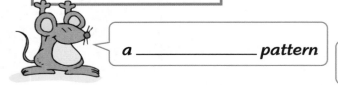

a _____ pattern

a _____ pattern

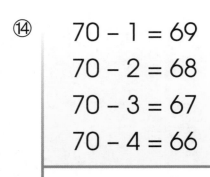

We can use an **equal sign** to show two number expressions that are equal.

e.g.

$$6 + 4 = 3 + 7$$

There are 10 beads in each group. "6 + 4" is equal to "3 + 7".

Circle the things. Then complete the expressions.

⑮

$$4 + \underline{\hspace{1cm}} = \underline{\hspace{1cm}} + \underline{\hspace{1cm}}$$

⑯

$$\underline{\hspace{1cm}} + 8 = \underline{\hspace{1cm}} + \underline{\hspace{1cm}}$$

Find the missing numbers.

⑰ $5 + 3 = 2 + \underline{\hspace{1cm}}$

⑱ $1 + 4 = \underline{\hspace{1cm}} + 3$

⑲ $9 + 7 = 8 + \underline{\hspace{1cm}}$

⑳ $6 + 5 = \underline{\hspace{1cm}} + 7$

㉑ $4 + 8 = \underline{\hspace{1cm}} + 2$

㉒ $3 + 9 = 6 + \underline{\hspace{1cm}}$

㉓

$$9 + 5 + 2 = 6 + 8 + \underline{\hspace{1cm}}$$

99, 89, 79, 69, 59,
49, 39, 29, 19, 9

Patterns (2)

- Find patterns in hundreds charts.
- Identify, describe, and extend a repeating pattern by combining two attributes.

Look at the hundreds chart. Complete the sentences with numbers and the given words.

row
column
growing
shrinking

1	2	3	4	5	6	7	⑧	9	10
11	12	13	14	15	16	17	⑱	19	20
21	22	23	24	25	26	27	㉘	29	30
31	32	33	34	35	36	37	㊳	39	40
41	42	43	44	45	46	47	㊽	49	50
51	52	53	54	55	56	57	㊽ 58	59	60
61	62	63	64	65	66	67	68	69	70
71	72	73	74	75	76	77	⑦⑧	79	80
81	82	83	84	85	86	87	⑧⑧	89	90
91	92	93	94	95	96	97	⑨⑧	99	100

① The coloured numbers are _____ .
They are in a _____ .

② The circled numbers are _____ .
They are in a _____ .

③ When we look at the numbers in a column from bottom to top, the numbers show a _____ pattern.

Complete the hundreds chart. Colour and circle the numbers on the hundreds chart. Then write "row" or "column" on the lines.

1	2	3			6			9	10
	12		14	15			18		20
21		23		25	26			29	
	32					37			
		43	44			47			50
51				55			58		
	62				66	67			70
71			74				78	79	
		83			86				
	92					97		99	

④ *Colour the numbers: 41, 42, 43, 44, 45, 46, 47, 48, 49, and 50.*

The coloured numbers are in a _____ .

⑤ *Circle the numbers: 3, 13, 23, 33, 43, 53, 63, 73, 83, and 93.*

The circled numbers are in a _____ .

Calculate and check ✔ the answers on the hundreds chart above. Then answer the questions.

⑥ 88 – 5 = _____

83 – 5 = _____

78 – 5 = _____

73 – 5 = _____

Do the answers follow a pattern? If they do, can you follow the pattern to find the answers of the next two subtraction sentences?

_____ ; _____

Colour the pictures as specified. Draw and colour the next picture. Then tell which attribute changes in each pattern apart from colour. Fill in the blanks with the given words.

pattern   position   shape   size

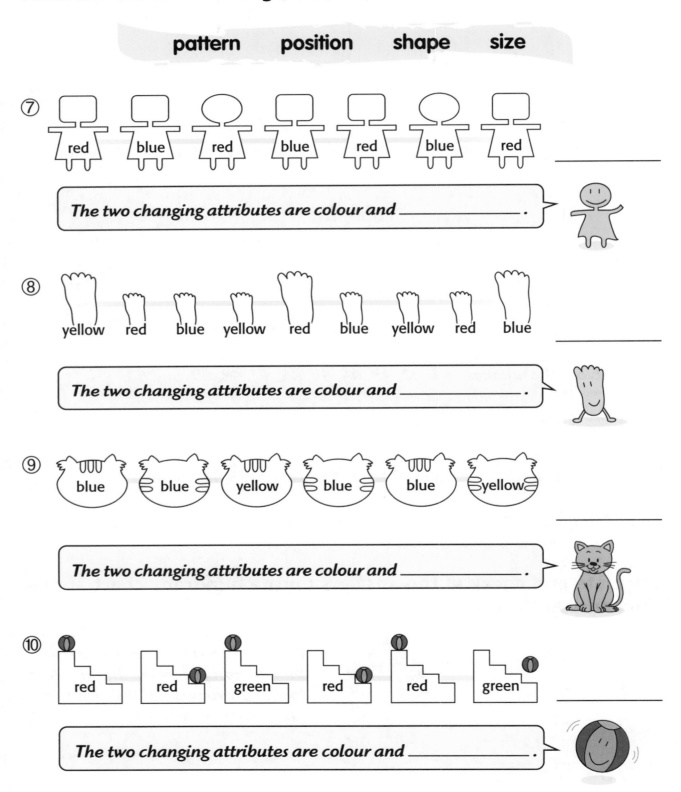

⑦ red blue red blue red blue red _____

The two changing attributes are colour and _____ .

⑧ yellow red blue yellow red blue yellow red blue _____

The two changing attributes are colour and _____ .

⑨ blue blue yellow blue blue yellow _____

The two changing attributes are colour and _____ .

⑩ red red green red red green _____

The two changing attributes are colour and _____ .

Find out which two attributes change in each pattern. Fill in the blanks with the given words.

colour   orientation   pattern   position   shape   size

⑪ _____

_____

⑫ _____

_____

⑬ _____

_____

⑭ _____

_____

Describe the pattern.

⑮

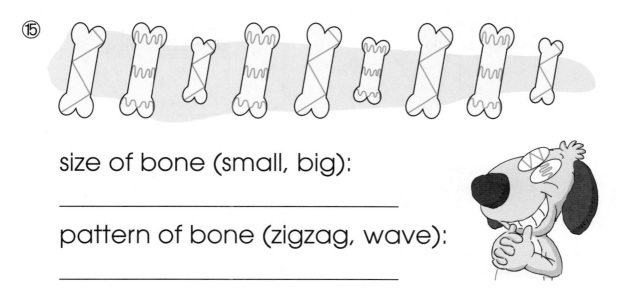

size of bone (small, big):

_____

pattern of bone (zigzag, wave):

_____

Organizing Data

- Organize objects into categories by sorting.
- Read and describe data presented in tally charts.
- Use tally charts to record data.

Sam, can you help me sort the buttons?

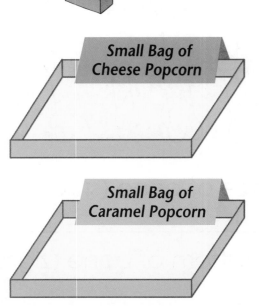

Sort the popcorn and write the letters on the correct trays.

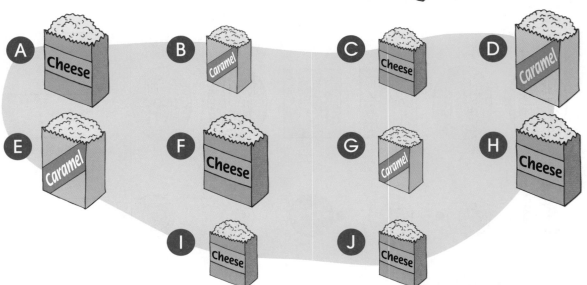

①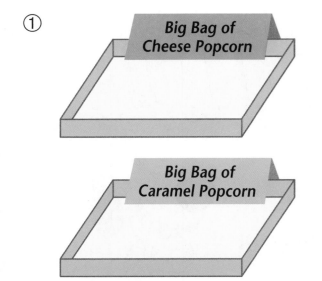

| Big Bag of Cheese Popcorn | Small Bag of Cheese Popcorn |
| Big Bag of Caramel Popcorn | Small Bag of Caramel Popcorn |

Colour each shape red or yellow. Then sort the shapes. Write the letters.

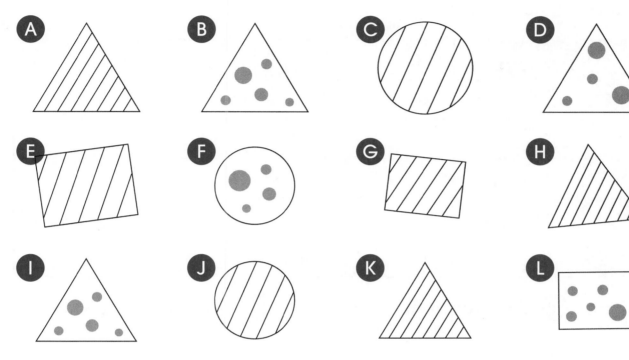

② **Red Shape with Stripes**	③ **Yellow Shape with Dots**
④ **Red Triangle with Dots**	⑤ **Yellow Circle with Stripes**

Mrs. Cowan numbered the children in her class from 1 to 16. Look at the record. Help her use tally marks (卌) to organize the data. Then answer the questions.

Jumper	Children	1	2	3	4	5	6	7	8	9	10	11	12	13	14	15	16
Style	With Hood	✔		✔	✔		✔		✔	✔		✔	✔			✔	
	Without Hood		✔			✔		✔			✔			✔	✔		✔
Colour	Black		✔		✔	✔			✔		✔						
	Blue	✔					✔			✔		✔				✔	✔
	Red			✔				✔					✔	✔	✔		

⑥

Ⓐ Jumper Style

With Hood: _____

Without Hood: _____

Ⓒ Type of Jumper

Black Jumper with Hood: _____

Blue Jumper with Hood: _____

Red Jumper with Hood: _____

Black Jumper without Hood: _____

Blue Jumper without Hood: _____

Red Jumper without Hood: _____

Ⓑ Jumper Colour

Black: _____

Blue: _____

Red: _____

Mrs. Cowan

⑦ *If I want to know the number of children wearing a jumper with hood, which card should I refer to?* ◯

⑧ *If I want to know the number of children wearing a red jumper without hood, which card should I refer to?* ◯

Colour each pair of shoes blue or brown. Then complete the table and use tally marks to show the data.

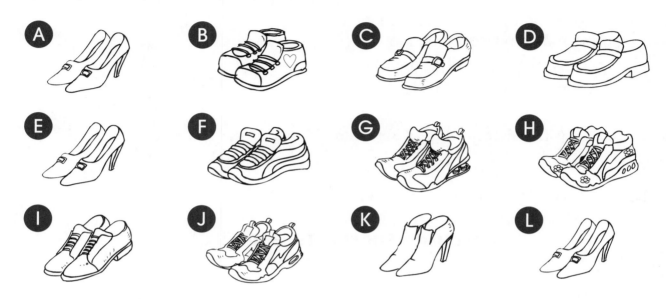

⑨

Shoes			A	B	C	D	E	F	G	H	I	J	K	L
Colour		Blue												
		Brown												
Type	Women's	With Shoelaces												
		Without Shoelaces												
	Men's	With Shoelaces												
		Without Shoelaces												

⑩ ## Men's Shoes

In blue, with shoelaces: _____

In blue, without shoelaces: _____

In brown, with shoelaces: _____

In brown, without shoelaces: _____

⑪ ## Women's Shoes

In blue, with shoelaces: _____

In blue, without shoelaces: _____

In brown, with shoelaces: _____

In brown, without shoelaces: _____

Pictographs

- Read pictographs and describe the data using mathematical language.
- Make pictographs to display data with appropriate titles and labels.

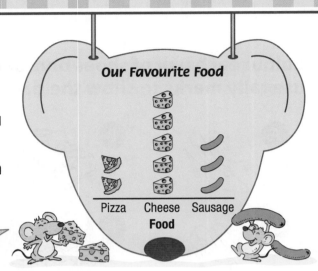

Our Favourite Food

Pizza   Cheese   Sausage

Food

> *Our favourite food is cheese.*

Look at the pictograph. Answer the questions.

Favourite Sports in Megan's Class

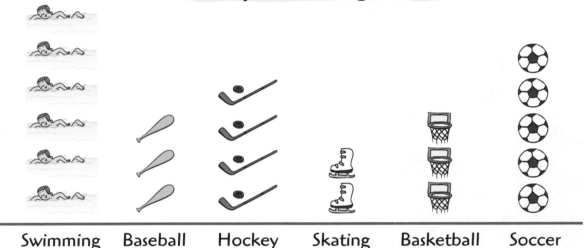

Swimming   Baseball   Hockey   Skating   Basketball   Soccer

Sports

① Which is the most popular sport? _____

② Which sport do fewer children like than baseball? _____

③ How many more children like soccer than basketball? ___ more

④ How many children are there in Megan's class? ___ children

Cathy and Tracy are counting their marbles. Look at the pictograph. Then answer the questions.

Cathy and Tracy's Marbles

Marbles

⑤ How many marbles with stripes do the girls have?   ___ marbles

⑥ How many marbles with a cat's eye do they have?   ___ marbles

⑦ How many kinds of marbles are there in all?   ___ kinds

⑧ Which kind of marble do they have the most?   _____

⑨

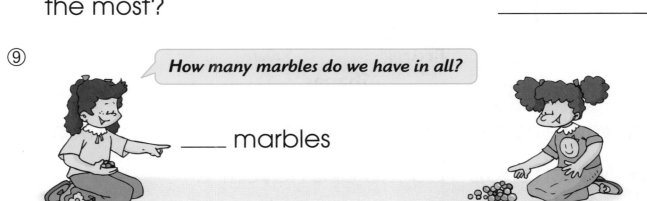

How many marbles do we have in all?

___ marbles

Read what the girls say. Help them complete the tally chart to record the number of shapes that they are going to make. Then complete the pictograph to show the data.

⑩

Shape	Number
Circle	‖
Rectangle	‖‖
Square	
Triangle	

I want to make 2 circles and 4 rectangles.

We're making 8 triangles and 3 squares.

I'm making 3 circles, 1 square, and 1 rectangle.

⑪ **Number of Shapes Made**

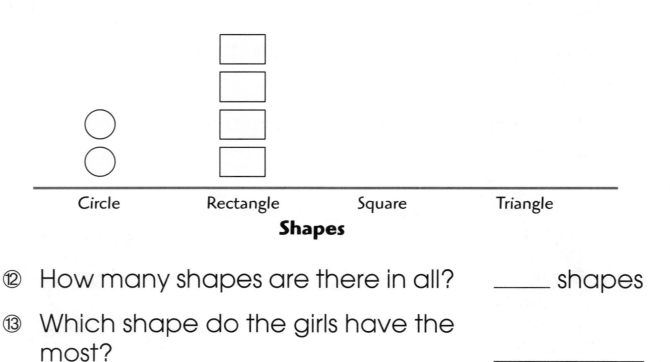

Circle   Rectangle   Square   Triangle

Shapes

⑫ How many shapes are there in all? _____ shapes

⑬ Which shape do the girls have the most? _____

Remember to give your pictograph a title and labels.

e.g.

Our Favourite Fruit ← title

Remember to align the pictures in each row.

Orange   Peach   Watermelon   Apple   Cherry ← labels

Fruit

See how many ice cream cones the children ate last month. Complete the pictograph and answer the questions.

Wayne: 6   Joe: 5   Ann: 3   Mary: 4   Tim: 1

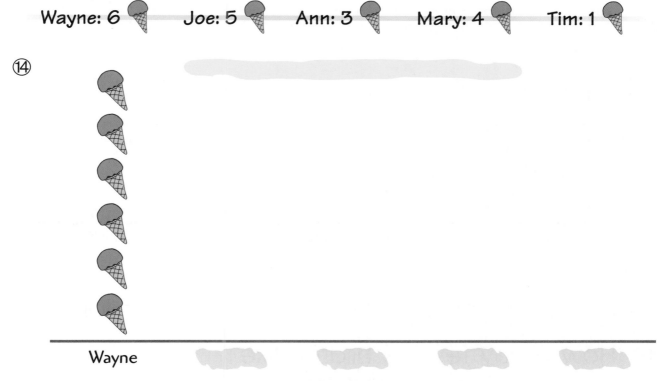

⑭

Wayne

Children

⑮

Who likes ice cream the most? Why?

_____

Bar Graphs

- Read and describe data presented in bar graphs.
- Complete or make bar graphs to show data.

James, don't you feel special being the only one in class who has a pet snake?

Yes, I do.

Look at the bar graph. Answer the questions.

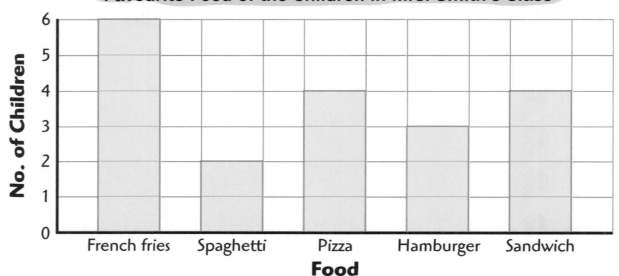

① How many children like pizza? ___ children

② How many fewer children like spaghetti than sandwich? ___ fewer

③ Which food is the most popular? _____

④ How many children are there in Mrs. Smith's class? ___ children

See how many boxes of doughnuts were sold at Mrs. Stanley's shop yesterday. Look at the graph. Then answer the questions.

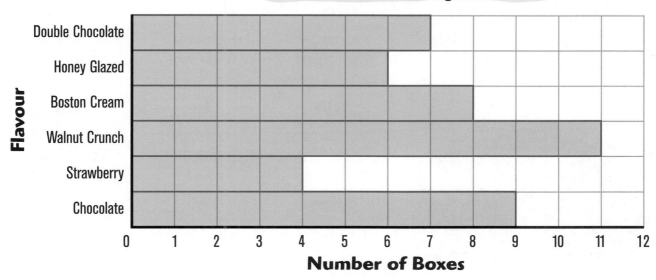

Number of Boxes of Doughnuts Sold

⑤ What is the title of the graph?

_____

⑥ Which flavour was the most popular?

_____

⑦ Which flavour was the least popular?

_____

⑧ *How many boxes of chocolate doughnuts were sold in all?*

_____ boxes

⑨ How many more boxes of Boston cream doughnuts than strawberry doughnuts were sold?

_____ more

See what the children want for lunch tomorrow. Record the orders with tally marks in ⑩ and check ✔ the letter in ⑪. Then complete the bar graph and answer the questions.

James
Hamburger
Salad

Gary
Chicken burger
French fries

Eva
Fish burger
French fries

Tina
Hamburger
Onion rings

Minnie
Hamburger
French fries

Katie
Fish burger
Onion rings

Joe
Hamburger
Salad

Louis
Chicken burger
Onion rings

Celine
Hamburger
French fries

David
Chicken burger
Salad

Ted
Hamburger
Onion rings

John
Hamburger
Onion rings

Derek
Fish burger
French fries

Wayne
Chicken burger
French fries

Lily
Fish burger
French fries

Ali
Hamburger
Salad

⑩

Sandwich	Number of Orders		Side Order	Number of Orders
Hamburger			Salad	
Chicken burger			French fries	
Fish burger			Onion rings	

⑪ Which is a better title for the following bar graph?

Ⓐ The Children's Lunch Tomorrow

Ⓑ The Children's Favourite Food

⑫

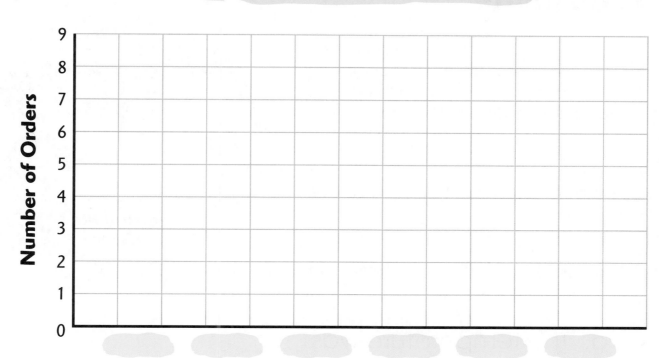

⑬ How many hamburgers will be ordered?

_____ hamburgers

⑭ How many orders of French fries will there be?

_____ orders

⑮ How many more hamburgers than fish burgers will be ordered?

_____ more

⑯ How many sandwiches will be ordered in all?

_____ sandwiches

Probability

- Use simple words such as "impossible", "unlikely", "less likely", "equally likely", "more likely", and "certain" to describe the probability that an event will occur.

Try again next time.

I bet she wants a necklace, which is impossible.

Use the given words to describe the situations.

impossible   unlikely   likely   certain

① a. The temperature was recorded in January. _____

b. The temperature was recorded in July. _____

② If you colour this picture,

a. you will get a dog. _____

b. you will get a coloured fish. _____

③ a. You can finish a box of muffins after dinner. 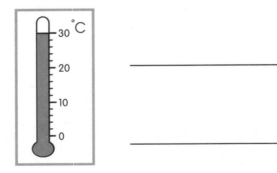 _____

b. A box of fresh muffins will go bad in an hour. _____

Look at the pictures. Then fill in the blanks with "less", "equally", or "more".

④ Maria will take a ball out of the bag without looking.

a. It is _____ likely to get a ball with dots or a ball with a number.

b. It is _____ likely to get a ball with stripes than a ball with dots.

⑤ Judy closes her eyes and picks an ice cream cone.

a. It is _____ likely to get a than a .

b. It is _____ likely to get a than a .

⑥ Peter is going to pick a box of juice.

a. It is _____ likely to pick a box of apple juice than a box of orange juice.

b. It is _____ likely to pick a box of grape juice than a box of apple juice.

Colour the pictures to match the sentences. Then fill in the blanks.

⑦

> These balls are either red or blue. If I pick one ball without looking, it is likely that I will get a red ball.

a.

b. It is more likely to get a _____ ball than a _____ ball.

⑧

> The flowers are yellow, red, or purple. The red flowers and the yellow flowers are the same in number. If I pick one flower without looking, it is likely that I will get a purple flower.

a.

b. It is equally likely to get a _____ flower or a _____ flower.

⑨

> My cards are yellow, green, or brown. Most of my cards are brown. If I turn over the cards and let Lucy take one, it is unlikely that she will get a yellow card.

a.

b. It is less likely to get a _____ card than a brown card.

Colour the spinners as specified. Then answer the questions.

⑩ 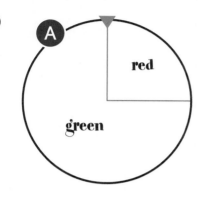 B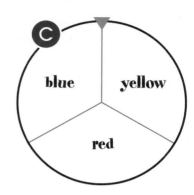

⑪ What colours will you get on each spinner?

A _____

B _____

C _____

⑫ Is it more likely to get green on **B** than **A** ? _____

⑬ Is it less likely to get blue on **B** than **C** ? _____

⑭ Is it equally likely to get red on **A** or **B** ? _____

⑮ For **C** , is it equally likely to get the three colours? _____

Read what Judy says. Help her draw lines and pictures on the spinner.

⑯ *I have a fair spinner. It is equally likely to land on*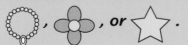

ENGLISH

Say It with Flowers

Flowers are a nice gift. Sometimes we can say things when we give someone flowers. Look at the flowers and their secret meanings:

Yellow Lily   "Thank you."
Sunflower   "I am proud of you."
Daisy   "I can keep a secret."
Apple Blossom   "I wish you good luck."
Purple Violet   "I think of you every day."
Forget-Me-Not   "Don't forget me."
White Lily   "You are sweet."
Red Rose   "I love you."

A. Read the passage and colour the flowers below.

1.

Thank you.

2.

I love you.

3.

I think of you every day.

B. Complete the crossword puzzle with the flower names from the passage.

Consonant Blends

Consonant blends are usually divided into the "l", "r", and "s" blends.

C. **Say the things in each group of pictures. Cross out ✗ the one that does not begin with the "l" blend.**

1. **bl** 　　

2. **cl** 　　

3. **fl** 　　

4. **gl** 　　

5. **pl** 　　

6. **sl** 　

D. **Circle the "r" blend words for the pictures in the word search.**

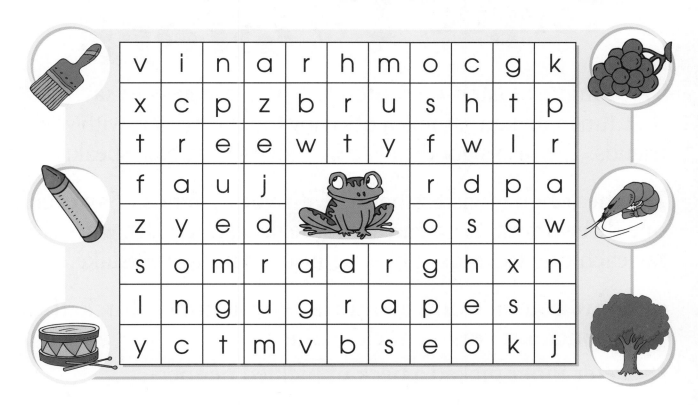

v	i	n	a	r	h	m	o	c	g	k
x	c	p	z	b	r	u	s	h	t	p
t	r	e	e	w	t	y	f	w	l	r
f	a	u	j				r	d	p	a
z	y	e	d				o	s	a	w
s	o	m	r	q	d	r	g	h	x	n
l	n	g	u	g	r	a	p	e	s	u
y	c	t	m	v	b	s	e	o	k	j

E. **Fill in the blanks with the correct "s" blends to complete the words.**

sc   sk   sm   sn   sp   st   sw

Mom bought a beautiful pot flower. It is 1._____arlet
and has a thick 2._____alk. It gives out a 3._____eet
scent. I helped Mom add some more soil to the pot
with a 4._____ade. Mom really loves the flower. She
5._____iles whenever she looks at it. I'm now making
a 6._____etch of the flower. I'm going to add a cute
7._____ail on one of the leaves.

Tongue Twisters

A tongue twister is a sentence that is not easy to say. It is fun to make a game out of saying tongue twisters with your friends. It is also a good way to improve the way we speak.

Try the tongue twisters below with your friends. Say each one three times. Who can say it the fastest? Or, see who can say each one the most times without making a mistake.

- How much wood would a woodchuck chuck if a woodchuck could chuck wood?
- Peter Piper picked a peck of pickled peppers.
- She sells seashells by the seashore.
- A big black bug bit a big black bear.
- I stopped at a fish sauce shop.

A.....bi...g...bla...ck....bu...g....
bi...t......a......bi...g......bl....a...
ck......be...a...r!

A. **Circle these words in the word search.**

woodchuck   picked   peck   pickled   peppers
sells   seashells   seashore   big   black   bug
bit   bear   stopped   fish   sauce   shop

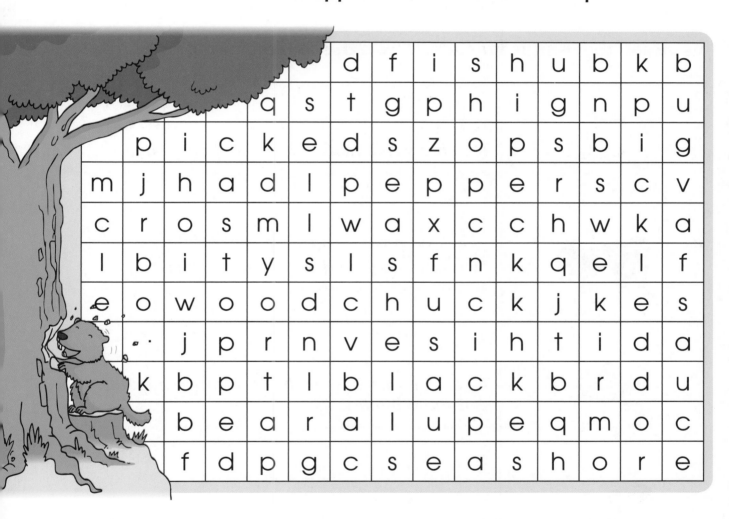

d	f	i	s	h	u	b	k	b
q	s	t	g	p	h	i	g	n	p	u
p	i	c	k	e	d	s	z	o	p	s	b	i	g
m	j	h	a	d	l	p	e	p	p	e	r	s	c	v
c	r	o	s	m	l	w	a	x	c	c	h	w	k	a
l	b	i	t	y	s	l	s	f	n	k	q	e	l	f
e	o	w	o	o	d	c	h	u	c	k	j	k	e	s
j	p	r	n	v	e	s	i	h	t	i	d	a
k	b	p	t	l	b	l	a	c	k	b	r	d	u
b	e	a	r	a	l	u	p	e	q	m	o	c
f	d	p	g	c	s	e	a	s	h	o	r	e

B. **Arrange the words in ( ) to form a tongue twister. Say it and ask your friends to try it.**

Which (wished   which   wicked   witch) wish?

_____

_____

Consonant Digraphs

"**Ch**", "**sh**", "**th**", and "**wh**" are **consonant digraphs**. They can be at the beginning, in the middle, or at the end of words.

Examples: tea<u>ch</u>er   fi<u>sh</u>   wi<u>th</u>out   <u>wh</u>iskers

C.   Read the tongue twisters.   Circle the consonant digraphs.

1.

   The cheery chipmunk chases the chubby child.

2.

   The sixth sheep cherishes the shiny shield.

3.

   Three thin thieves stole the fifth feather from the thoughtful brother.

4.

   The witty whale wonders whether the wheel will whirl round the withered wheat.

5.

   We shall sew and sell sheets in the shabby shack.

D. Put the words with consonant digraphs in (C) in the correct boxes.

The Tomatina
– the Strangest Festival in the World

The Tomatina is a very strange festival held every year in Buñol, Spain. It started as a joke among some people in this small town about 70 years ago, but now people from all over the world come to join in the fun.

So what is the fun all about? The people of Buñol put on a food fight! On the last Wednesday in August, when the tomatoes that are grown all around the town are ready to be picked, truckloads of ripe, red tomatoes are brought to the town centre. Then, for two hours, everyone throws tomatoes at one another! Everyone is laughing and having a good time being naughty! There is a lot of partying in the days before and after this great food fight festival.

A. Circle the words that are related to the Tomatina.

April   food fight   Sunday

Spain   tomatoes   August

festival   Buñol   red peppers

parties   Wednesday   town centre

B. Match the two parts. Write the letters on the lines.

A the length of time the food fight lasts

B where the food fight takes place

C when the festival started

D a small town in Spain

1. the town centre of Buñol   ____

2. Buñol   ____

3. about 70 years ago   ____

4. two hours   ____

Silent Consonants

Some **consonants** like "**b**", "**g**", "**gh**", "**h**", "**k**", "**l**", "**n**", "**c**", "**t**", and "**w**" are silent in some words.

Examples: fi<u>gh</u>t   <u>h</u>eir   colum<u>n</u>

C. **Say these words with silent consonants. Write them under the correct pictures.**

| thum**b** | slei**gh** | **gh**ost | **k**not |
| pa**l**m | s**c**issors | lis**t**en | s**w**ord |

1.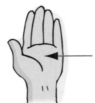

_____

2.

_____

3.

_____

4.

_____

5.

_____

6.

_____

7.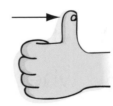

_____

8.

_____

D. Say each word. Circle the silent consonant. Write another word with the same silent consonant.

> *One of the words has more than one silent consonant.*

1. castle

2. stalk

3. gnaw

4. two

5. autumn

6. hour

7. climb

8. science

9. knight

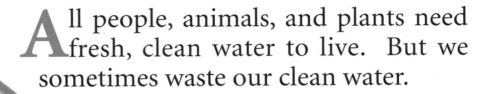

All people, animals, and plants need fresh, clean water to live. But we sometimes waste our clean water.

There are many things we can do to protect our supply of fresh, clean water. Make sure that the kitchen sink tap is not running when you help wash the dishes. Put a plug in the kitchen sink and fill it with water instead.

You can also save water in the bathroom. Try this: fill a glass with water. Then shut off the tap. Wet your toothbrush. Brush your teeth. Then use the water in the glass to rinse your mouth. Pour the rest of the water over your toothbrush to rinse it off.

It is important to take care of our fresh water supply. Let's save water. Let's not waste it.

A. Check ✔ the ways of saving water at home.

1. Fill the kitchen sink with water and wash the dishes with the water.

2. Do not water your plants.

3. Shut off the tap when you are brushing your teeth.

4. Drink less water.

5. Do not make ice cubes with water.

6. Do not leave the tap running when you are washing the dishes.

B. Write one more way of saving water at home. Draw a picture to go with it.

Short and Long Vowels

Some words with the letters a, e, i, o, or u have the **short vowel sounds**. Some words with these letters have the **long vowel sounds**. Long vowel sounds sound the same as the way you say the letters.

Examples: Short vowel – c<u>a</u>p
Long vowel – c<u>a</u>pe

C. **Fill in the missing letters to complete the words. Say the words. Write them in the correct pots.**

gl__ss   br__sh   f__ve

h__lp   s__ve   __se

__cean   f__sh   p__t

Short Vowel

Long Vowel

D. **Say the things in the bubbles. Find the words in the word search. Colour the short-vowel words yellow and the long-vowel words pink.**

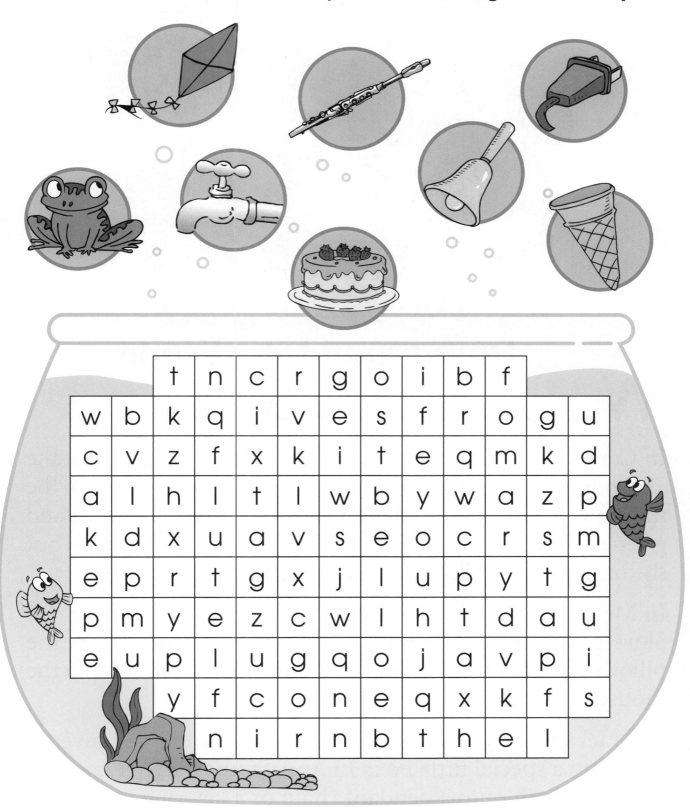

	t	n	c	r	g	o	i	b	f		
w	b	k	q	i	v	e	s	f	r	o	g	u
c	v	z	f	x	k	i	t	e	q	m	k	d
a	l	h	l	t	l	w	b	y	w	a	z	p
k	d	x	u	a	v	s	e	o	c	r	s	m
e	p	r	t	g	x	j	l	u	p	y	t	g
p	m	y	e	z	c	w	l	h	t	d	a	u
e	u	p	l	u	g	q	o	j	a	v	p	i
	y	f	c	o	n	e	q	x	k	f	s
	n	i	r	n	b	t	h	e	l

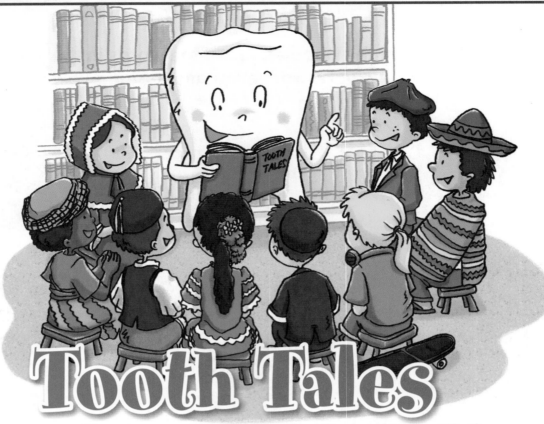

Tooth Tales
from around the World

What happens in your family when you lose a tooth?

In Canada and the United States we hope for a visit from the Tooth Fairy. We put our tooth under our pillow at night. In the morning, we see that the Tooth Fairy has taken our tooth and given us some money. In France, the Tooth Fairy also visits, but she may give the children a small toy instead of money.

In Mexico and Spain, children get money from a mouse! In Slovenia, the mouse takes the tooth and puts candy under the pillow. In Nigeria, the child hides the tooth in the attic, so the mouse does not find it!

In Israel and Italy, they just keep the baby tooth as a souvenir, maybe in a special little box. In Austria, the parents may put the baby tooth onto a pendant chain or a key ring.

A. **Match the countries with the tooth tales. Write the letters in the boxes.**

A The child gets money from a mouse.

B The child keeps the tooth as a souvenir.

C The child gets a small toy from the Tooth Fairy.

D The child gets candy from a mouse.

E The child gets some money from the Tooth Fairy.

F The parents put the tooth onto a pendant chain or a key ring.

G The child hides the tooth in the attic.

1. Canada
   United States ☐

2. Israel
   Italy ☐

3. France ☐

4. Austria ☐

5. Slovenia ☐

6. Mexico
   Spain ☐

7. Nigeria ☐

Vowel Diphthongs

The "**oi**" as in "boil", "**oy**" as in "boy", "**ou**" as in "out", and "**ow**" as in "now" are **vowel diphthongs**.

B. **Say the words in the toy box. Colour the words with vowel diphthongs.**

cousin	toy	brown
join	bowl	our
doing	soup	soil
mouth	point	joy
snow	voice	going
foyer	count	shower
wow	four	own

C. **Say the things.   Write the letters in the correct places.**

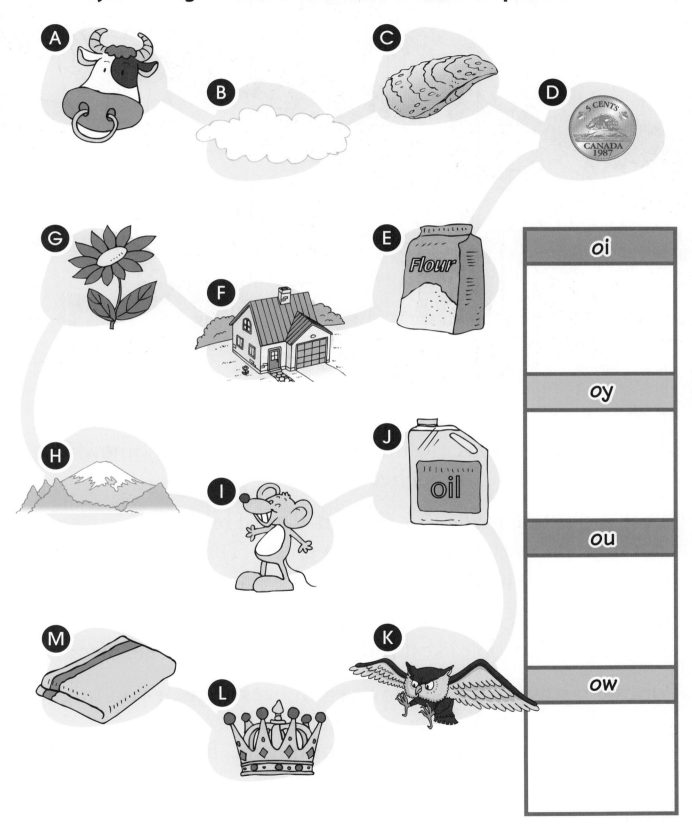

oi
oy
ou
ow

Mmmmm... Poutine!

Have you ever eaten poutine? Poutine is a very Canadian fast food. It was invented about 60 years ago, somewhere in the countryside of Quebec.

What is poutine made of ? It is made of French fries covered with fresh cheese curds and brown gravy. The hot gravy melts the cheese curds to make poutine a very tasty – and gooey – treat!

People in other countries are now trying poutine. In Italy, for example, some people like it with spaghetti sauce instead of gravy.

Poutine tastes great. But don't eat it every day or you might get fat. And be careful when you eat it because it is messy! You can eat plain French fries with your fingers. But when you eat poutine, it is a good idea to use a fork.

Yum!

A. Read the passage. Circle the correct answers.

1. Poutine was invented about ___ years ago.

   40   50   60

2. It was invented in ___ .

   Quebec   Ontario   Alberta

3. Poutine is French fries with ___ and hot gravy.

   bean curds   butter curds   cheese curds

4. People in Italy eat poutine with ___ .

   sour cream   salad dressing   spaghetti sauce

5. You use a ___ to eat poutine.

   spoon   knife   fork

B. Find words from the passage to replace the underlined words.

1. The poutine is <u>delicious</u>.   _____

2. I have never <u>tried</u> poutine before.   _____

3. Melted cheese is <u>sticky</u>.   _____

4. The table becomes <u>dirty</u> after each meal.   _____

Long Vowel Digraphs

Sometimes two letters form a long vowel sound. It is called a **long vowel digraph**.

"**Ai**", "**ay**", "**ei**", "**ea**", "**ee**", "**oa**", "**ow**", "**oo**", "**ew**", "**au**", and "**aw**" are all long vowel digraphs.

Examples: <u>ei</u>ght   l<u>ea</u>f   sn<u>ow</u>

C. Say the things. Circle the correct long vowel digraphs.

1.

ee / ei

2.

oa / oo

3.

ai / ea

4.

aw / ew

5.

aw / ow

6.

ai / ee

7.

au / ay

8.

au / ay

9.

ew / oa

D. Circle the words with long vowel digraphs.

1. They put the poutine on the tray.

2. It is one of my favourite treats.

3. Can I have poutine on toast?

4. My sister likes plain French fries instead.

5. She does not like anything gooey.

E. Write as many words with long vowel digraphs as you can with the given letters.

1. b__ __

2. p__ __l

3. d__ __r

4. tr__ __

5. r__ __d

6. h__ __l

Kelly's Broken Wrist

My big sister Kelly fell off her bicycle on the weekend. Luckily, she was wearing a helmet. She did not hurt her head. But she did break her wrist.

My dad and I took my sister to the hospital. A man at the hospital took an X-ray of Kelly's wrist. Then another person put a plaster cast on her wrist. Kelly said I could write something on her new cast. I was the first person to sign my name on it. I drew a happy face too, with coloured felt pens.

I think Kelly is brave. She did not cry. When Kelly goes skateboarding, though, she always wears a helmet, wrist guards, elbow pads, and knee pads.

It is important to protect ourselves when we play sports.

A. Kelly is skateboarding. Write what she is wearing.

1.

2.

3.

4.

B. Read the story and answer the questions.

1. How did Kelly get hurt?

_____

2. Who took an X-ray of Kelly's wrist?

_____

3. What did the writer do on the plaster cast?

_____

_____

R-controlled Vowels

R-controlled vowels are vowels with the "r" sound. "**Ar**", "**er**", "**ir**", "**or**", and "**ur**" are R-controlled vowels.

Examples: p<u>er</u>son   d<u>ir</u>ty   h<u>or</u>se

C. **Kelly is lost in the park. Help her get out of the park by circling the words with R-controlled vowels.**

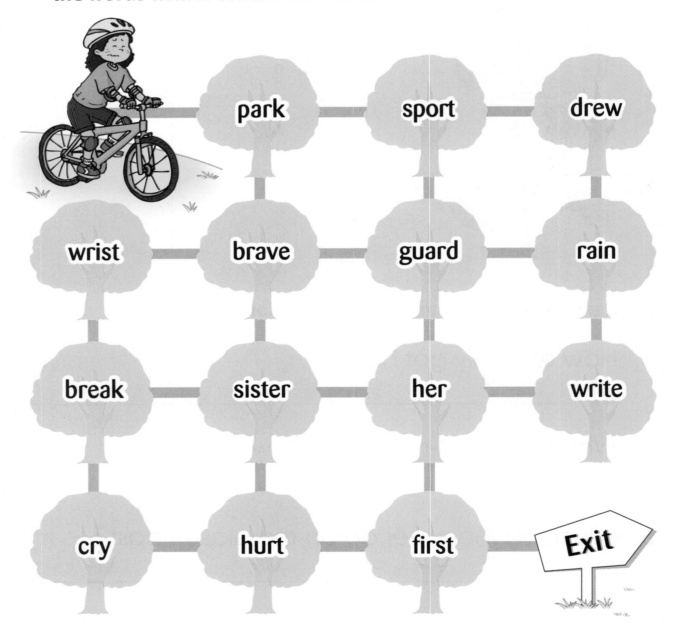

park	sport	drew
wrist	brave	guard	rain
break	sister	her	write
cry	hurt	first	Exit

D.   Say the things.   Write the letters in the correct places.

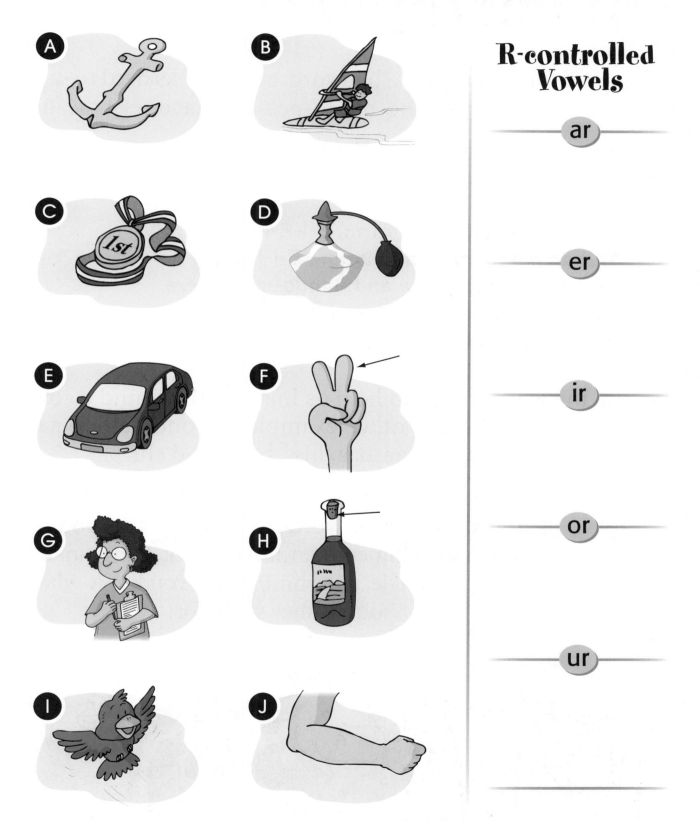

R-controlled Vowels

ar _____

er _____

ir _____

or _____

ur _____

_____

Onomatopoeia

Onomatopoeia is such a big word, and it looks hard to say. We say it like this: o-no-ma-to-pee-a. What does it mean?

Onomatopoeia are words that sound like the things they describe. Sing this song:

Old Macdonald had a farm, E-I-E-I-O.
And on his farm he had a cow, E-I-E-I-O.
With a moo-moo here and a moo-moo there.
Here a moo, there a moo, everywhere a moo-moo.
Old Macdonald had a farm, E-I-E-I-O.

We use the word "moo" to help us imagine the sound a cow makes! Here are some other examples of onomatopoeia: quack, bow-wow, baa-baa, hiss, buzz, and chirp.

But we do not use such words only to talk about animal sounds. Say these words: squeak, splash, boom, crash, rustle, chime, groan, hiccup, click, clang, tinkle, jingle, and rumble. Do you know what sounds they stand for?

A. Write the onomatopoeia under the correct pictures.

hiss
buzz
click
chirp
tinkle
rustle
chime
quack
splash
rumble

1.

_____

2.

_____

3.

_____

4.

_____

5.

_____

6.

_____

7.

_____

8.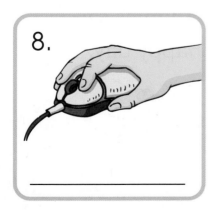

_____

9.

_____

10.

_____

Rhyming Words

Rhyming words are words that have the same ending sound.

Examples: b<u>ean</u>   gr<u>een</u>

A rhyme has lines ending in rhyming pairs.

B. Read the rhyme. Circle the rhyming pairs at the end of the lines with different colours.

The dog says "woof"
As he waves to the squirrel on the roof

The duck says "quack"
And the frog hops onto his back.

The bird says "tweet"
As she kicks her little feet.

The cow says "moo"
To the flies he wants to shoo.

The cat says "purr"
When the girl gently touches her fur.

Listen to what the animals say
And enjoy a great happy day.

C. **Draw a line to match each rhyming pair. Write one more word that rhymes with them.**

1. hour •

2. break •

3. whether •

4. beak •

5. cable •

6. bought •

7. care •

8. aisle •

9. eight •

10. store •

• **A** stable

• **B** fair

• **C** steak

• **D** caught

• **E** flour

• **F** straight

• **G** seek

• **H** door

• **I** feather

• **J** style

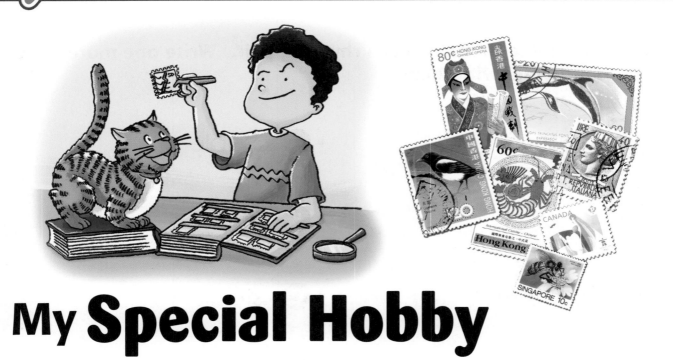

My Special Hobby

I have a special hobby. It is stamp collecting. My father used to collect stamps. He gave me his stamp albums. I have been collecting stamps for two years. I have many stamp albums now!

I have stamps from many different places. My mother's cousins live in China. They send me beautiful stamps from that country. My friend Tara moved to Italy last year. She sends me stamps, too. At Christmas time, we get many cards. I cut the stamps off the envelopes and put them in my albums.

Some stamps are big. Some are small. Some have pictures. Some have photographs. The stamps can be pictures of anything: people, animals, and flowers. I got a stamp from Hong Kong. It had different kinds of bread on it.

I enjoy collecting stamps. Some day I will give my collection to my own children.

A. Read the clues. Complete the crossword puzzle.

Across

A. something you do for pleasure

B. You send letters or cards in them.

C. deliver

Down

1. not the same

2. You need a camera to take them.

3. not common

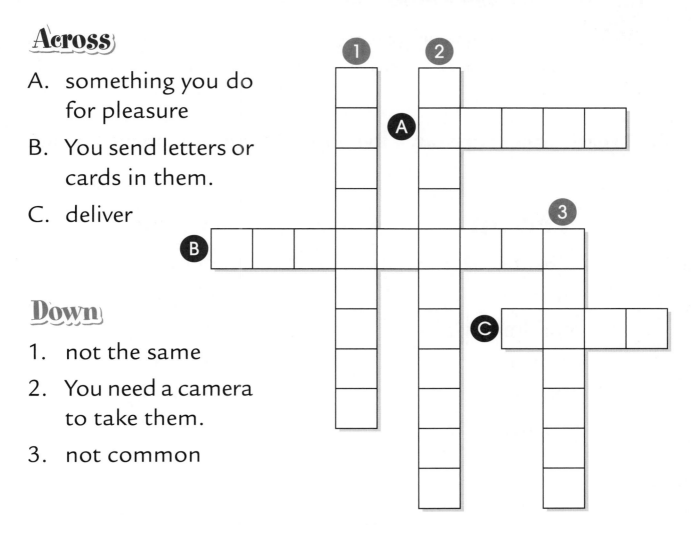

B. Design your own stamp. Colour it. Write a sentence about your stamp.

_____

_____

Common Nouns

A **common noun** names any person, animal, place, or thing.

Examples: aunt   beaver   mall   album

C. In each group, cross out ✗ the words that are not common nouns.

Person
Sean
friend
children
cousins
Karen
father

Animal
Pug
kitten
goose
Nemo
tiger
dog

Place
country
school
Lake Simcoe
Hong Kong
theatre
airport

Thing
bread
stamp
photographs
PlayStation
Barbie
cards

Proper Nouns

A **proper noun** names a specific person, animal, place, or thing. It always begins with a capital letter. Days of the week, months of the year, and festival names are proper nouns.

Examples: Melissa   Bambi   Hamilton   Easter

D.   Rewrite the sentences correctly.

1.   My friend tara has moved to italy.

_____

_____

2.   I received a christmas card from her last monday.

_____

_____

3.   The stamp has a golden retriever on it.

_____

_____

4.   tara will come back to toronto for a visit in july.

_____

_____

Berry Time

Raspberries in the bushes
Blueberries on the ground
Summertime is berry time
Look at what I've found!

Strawberries! Chokecherries! Cranberries!
Don't forget the saskatoons!
I love picking berries
I love to eat them, too!

In jams and pies and cobblers
Alone or with some cream
Wash them well, no need to waste
They're the sweetest jewels you'll ever taste!

Summertime is berry time
A very merry berry time!

A. **Match the names with the pictures. Write the letters. Then name one more berry and draw a picture to go with it.**

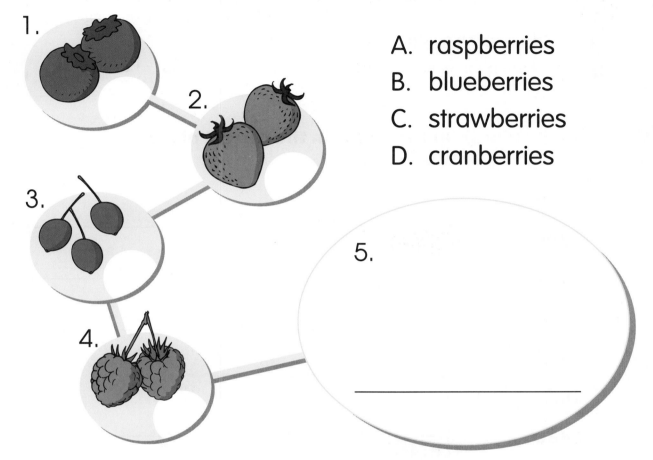

A. raspberries

B. blueberries

C. strawberries

D. cranberries

1.

2.

3.

4.

5. _____

B. **Colour the 🍓 if the sentences are true.**

1. Raspberries grow in trees.

2. We pick berries in summer.

3. We can make pies with berries.

4. We should wash berries before we eat them.

5. Jewels are sweet.

Plural Nouns

Add "s" or "es" to most nouns to form **plurals**. For nouns ending in "y", change the "y" to "i" and add "es".

Examples: clock → clocks   brush → brushes   daisy → daisies

C. **Write the plurals of the words in the correct places.**

city
bus
box
lily
wish
baby
peach
basket
bench
cartoon
lollipop
puppy
rainbow
butterfly
season

s

jewels

_____ _____

_____ _____

es

bushes

_____ _____

_____ _____

ies

blueberries

_____ _____

_____ _____

Compound Words

A **compound word** is formed when two words are put together to form a new word of a different meaning.

Example: gold + fish → goldfish

D. Look at the picture clues and circle the compound words in the word search.

d	m	g	y	l	u	n	o	k	h
f	q	p	f	i	r	e	f	l	y
i	a	r	v	g	l	b	w	q	t
y	x	s	p	h	s	o	m	w	c
b	c	t	q	t	u	v	o	a	q
o	e	a	c	h	m	z	d	l	h
h	l	r	s	o	m	a	x	e	l
k	z	f	j	u	e	j	r	u	g
s	w	i	h	s	r	z	p	m	r
b	a	s	k	e	t	b	a	l	l
i	r	h	o	s	i	x	w	t	f
e	u	n	t	y	m	v	d	j	s
t	h	o	r	s	e	s	h	o	e
l	c	v	g	r	n	i	p	b	k

Who Invented the Sandwich?

Schoolchildren often eat sandwiches. But have you ever wondered who thought of putting food in between two slices of bread?

Some people think it was a man named John Montagu. He was an English nobleman who lived about 250 years ago. He had a special title: the Fourth Earl of Sandwich. Sandwich is the name of a town in England.

This man loved to play card games. Once, he was so busy playing cards that he did not want to stop to eat. He asked the cook to put some meat between two pieces of bread so he could eat and play cards at the same time. So, John Montagu ate the world's first sandwich.

The people of France do not believe this story. They say that French farm workers and travellers often prepared meat or fish between two slices of bread. But they did not have a special name for it.

A. Look at the picture clues. Complete the crossword puzzle.

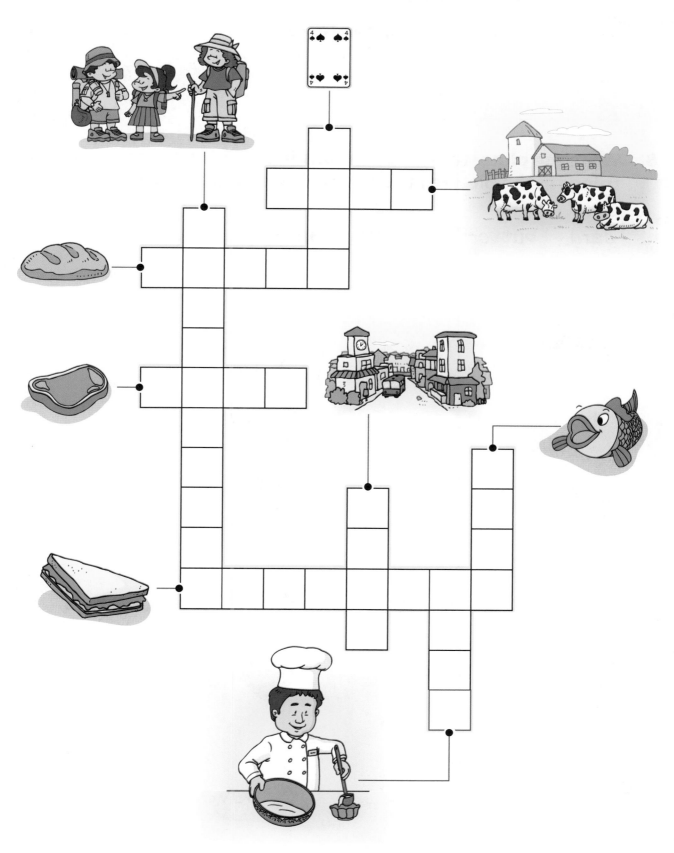

Countable Nouns

Some nouns are **countable**. Number words can be used before their plural form to show the quantity.

Example: eight pencils

B. Write the plural form of the nouns in the correct places. Add the things in the pictures to show the correct quantities.

card   butterfly   heart   sandwich   carrot   ball

1. two _____

2. three _____

3. four _____

4. five _____

5. six _____

6. seven _____

Uncountable Nouns

Some nouns are **uncountable**. They do not have any plural form, and number words cannot be used before them.

Example: beef (✔)   two beefs (✘)

C. Colour the uncountable nouns.

farm   piece   man   meat   game

bread   town   ice   sugar   story

year   wool   meal   rain   glue

D. Circle the correct words to complete the sentences.

1. Do you want butter / butters in your sandwich?

2. Can I have one more lollipop / bubble gums ?

3. We need to buy some milk / milks .

4. Don't add salt / salts in the tea / teas .

5. I've got five money / dollars .

Brother Moon
and *Sister Sun*
– an Inuit Legend

One night there was a drum dance. A young girl stayed at home alone. Someone came in, blew out the light, and pulled the girl's hair. The person ran away before the girl had a chance to see who it was.

The young girl wanted to find out who pulled her hair. She put some ashes on her hair and waited.

The visitor came back, pulled the girl's hair again, and ran away. The girl went quickly to the dance hall. She saw that her brother had ashes on his hands. The girl was angry. She grabbed a torch and ran away. Her brother grabbed his own torch and followed her into the dark night. He wanted to say sorry. They both ran so fast that they took off into the sky.

The girl became the sun and her brother, whose torch went out, became the moon.

A.   Unscramble the letters and write the opposites of these words.

 bright
a k d r
_____

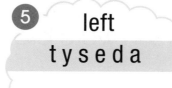 pushed
l u l e p d
_____

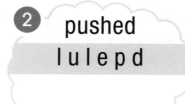 day
t i g h n
_____

 slowly
c q k i y u l
_____

left
t y s e d a
_____

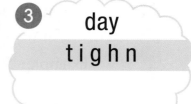 happy
r a g n y
_____

B.   Check ✔ the correct sentence in each pair.

1. ☐ A   There was a drum dance in the morning.

    ☐ B   There was a drum dance at night.

2. ☐ A   Someone blew out the light.

    ☐ B   Someone lit the light.

3. ☐ A   The girl put ashes on her hair.

    ☐ B   The girl put her hair on some ashes.

4. ☐ A   The girl became the moon.

    ☐ B   The girl became the sun.

Telling Sentences

A **telling sentence** tells about someone or something. It begins with a capital letter and ends with a period (.).

Example: She has long hair.

C.   Colour the ☼ for telling sentences.

1. The moon and the sun were brother and and sister.

2. The boy liked playing tricks on his sister.

3. Was she angry?

4. You naughty boy!

5. Stop running, please.

6. Don't follow me!

7. The boy felt sorry for what he did.

8. Oh, my torch has gone out!

9. He became the moon.

D. Put the words in order to form telling sentences.

1. is   sun   brightly   the   shining

_____

2. look   the   we   at   sun   cannot   directly

_____

3. can   we   full   tonight   see   moon   the

_____

4. it   shiny   is   a   mirror   like   round

_____

E. Write three telling sentences about the picture.

1. _____

2. _____

3. _____

Chinese Birth Signs

Maybe you have heard of *Gemini* or *Aquarius* or *Libra*. These are our birth signs. What our birth sign is depends on the month of our birth. Some people use these signs to read their horoscopes every day. Their horoscopes tell them their future.

There is something much like this in China. But there, the year when we are born tells us our birth sign. These birth signs are 12 animals. Look at the list below to see what animal you are:

2008 – Rat	2009 – Ox	2010 – Tiger
2011 – Rabbit	2012 – Dragon	2013 – Snake
2014 – Horse	2015 – Sheep	2016 – Monkey
2017 – Rooster	2018 – Dog	2019 – Pig

Do you believe in birth signs?

A. Write the Chinese birth signs the pictures show.

2008

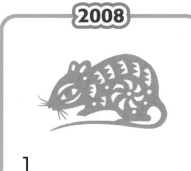

1. _____

2009

2. _____

2010

3. _____

2011

4. _____

2012

5. _____

2013

6. _____

2014

7. _____

2015

8. _____

2016

9. _____

2017

10. _____

2018

11. _____

2019

12. _____

Asking Sentences

An **asking sentence** asks about someone or something. It begins with a capital letter and ends with a question mark (?).

Example: Can you tell me your birth sign?

B. Fill in the blanks to complete the asking sentences.

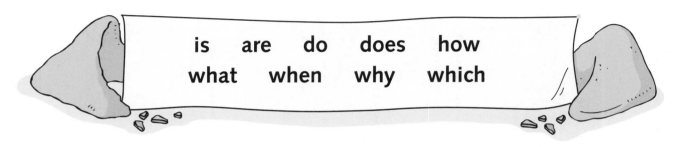

is   are   do   does   how
what   when   why   which

1. _____ you know your birth sign?

2. In _____ year were you born?

3. _____ your mother believe in birth signs?

4. _____ many Chinese birth signs are there?

5. _____ Cat one of the Chinese birth signs?

6. _____ is the birth sign of a girl born in 2015?

7. _____ you a Gemini?

8. _____ are people interested in horoscopes?

9. _____ did you start reading your horoscope?

C. Write the asking sentences correctly.

1. can you draw your birth sign

    _____

2. where can we learn about horoscopes

    _____

    _____

3. do horoscopes really tell us our future

    _____

    _____

D. Read the answers and complete the asking sentences.

1. Which _____

    _____

    The birth sign Dragon comes after Rabbit.

2. Is _____

    Yes, Rat is the first birth sign on the list.

3. What _____

    I would like to add Panda to the list.

Billy's Bad Dream

Billy:

I had a bad dream, Mom! I dreamed that I was lost in a jungle. It was dark and there were vines everywhere.

I saw a vine hanging in front of me. Suddenly the vine moved. It was a snake! I ran as fast as I could. Then a monkey flew by. It swooped down and stole my banana!

I was hungry. I saw a bush with big, red berries on them. But when I reached to take one, they all flew away. I thought they were flying spiders! I started to shout, and then you woke me up.

Mom:

Don't worry, Billy. You are safe with me, and you are not in a scary jungle any more. But I think I know why you had this bad dream.

Billy:

Why, Mom?

Mom:

Do you remember what bedtime story I read to you last night? It was called The Scary Jungle Book!

A.   Read about Billy's dream. Check ✔ the correct picture in each pair.

1.

2.

3.

4.

Surprising Sentences

A **surprising sentence** shows a strong feeling like fear, anger, or excitement. It begins with a capital letter and ends with an exclamation mark (!).

Example: What a nightmare!

B. Write the numbers for the surprising sentences in the monster's bag.

1. I had a dream last night.

2. Wow, it's so dark here!

3. What a big monster!

4. What is it carrying?

5. Oh, no! It can fly!

6. Help!

7. Can somebody help me?

8. How scary!

C. **Match the surprising sentences with what they say. Write the letters.**

> **A. Yummy!**   **B. Boo!**
> **C. What a huge bear!**   **D. Oh, no!**

D. **Look at each picture. Write a surprising sentence to go with it.**

1. _____

2. _____

3. _____

S'mores!

A s'more is the gooiest, tastiest, best campfire treat! Once you have built your campfire, making s'mores is quite easy. First, you get two graham crackers and put them on a plate. Next, you place a small square of your favourite chocolate onto one of the graham crackers.

Then you put a big marshmallow on a long stick and hold it over the flame of the campfire. Be careful now! You want the marshmallow to turn golden brown and not get burned.

Then, when the marshmallow is done, take it off your stick and place it on top of the chocolate square. Finally, put the second graham cracker on top of the marshmallow and press down gently. It's time to eat...delicious!

S'more is a strange word. What does it mean? Well, if you eat one, you are going to want...some more. S'more!

A. Colour the things you need to make s'mores.

B. Put the sentences in order. Write them on the lines below.

- Heat a marshmallow over a campfire.
- Put a chocolate square on a graham cracker.
- Put another graham cracker on top.
- Enjoy the s'more!
- Place the marshmallow on the chocolate square.

1. _____

2. _____

3. _____

4. _____

5. _____

Imperative Sentences

An **imperative sentence** tells someone to do or not to do something. It begins with a capital letter and ends with a period (.). The subject "you" is left out.

Examples: Write the answer in your book.

Don't tell anyone about it.

C. Check ✔ the imperative sentences.

1. Have you made s'mores before?

2. Don't sit too close to the campfire.

3. Pass me the marshmallows, please.

4. Heat it over the flame until it turns brown.

5. Try it.

6. Wow, it's great!

7. It's easy to make.

8. Would you like some more?

9. Don't forget to put out the fire.

D. Write the imperative sentences correctly.

1. turn down the volume

_____

2. put away your books

_____

3. just leave it there, Cedric

_____

4. don't throw it away

_____

E. Write an imperative sentence for each situation.

1. You want your sister Jane to feed the fish.

_____

2. You want your friend to meet you at the theatre.

_____

3. You remind your brother not to ride his bike on the road.

_____

_____

How Canada Got Its Name

It is fun to learn the meanings of country names. For example, China means "middle kingdom" and Japan means "origin of the sun". The name Namibia comes from the word "namib" which means "area where there is nothing".

So what does Canada mean? How did our country get its name?

The name Canada may have come from the First Nations word "kanata" meaning "village" or "group of huts". When the first explorers from France and England came here, they heard the Iroquois people use this word.

In 1867, there was a meeting in London, England to choose the name of the new country made up of Quebec, Ontario, Nova Scotia, and New Brunswick. There were many ideas, but the name Canada was finally chosen. Do you like this choice?

A.   Draw lines to match the country names with their meanings.

 Canada •

 China •

 Japan •

 Namibia •

• origin of the sun

• village

• area where there is nothing

• middle kingdom

B.   Colour the 🍁 if the sentences are true.

1.   Namibia is a country.

2.   "Kanata" is a First Nations word.

3.   People from England and Japan were among the first explorers in Canada.

4.   The name Canada was chosen in 1867 for the new country.

5.   Quebec, Ontario, Nova Scotia, and London made up the new country.

Subjects

A sentence has two main parts – a subject and a predicate.

The **subject** tells whom or what the sentence is about.

Example: The maple <u>trees</u> are tall.

C. Circle the subject of each sentence.

1. The name of our country comes from a First Nations word.

2. Canada is a big country.

3. People in Canada are from different cultures.

4. The beaver is one of the symbols of Canada.

5. Ottawa is the capital city.

6. Colourful tulips bloom all over the city in May.

7. Tourists like visiting the Parliament Buildings.

8. The summer in Canada is warm with plenty of sunshine.

Predicates

The **predicate** of a sentence tells what the subject is or what the subject does.

Example: All of us <u>love maple syrup</u>.

D.   Underline the predicate of each sentence.

1.   My family came to Canada five years ago.

2.   We lived in Montreal at first.

3.   We moved here last year.

4.   I go to Westland School.

5.   I have made many new friends.

6.   I always send e-mail to my friends in Montreal.

7.   I miss them.

8.   Dennis said he might come to visit me this summer.

Scotty the T. Rex

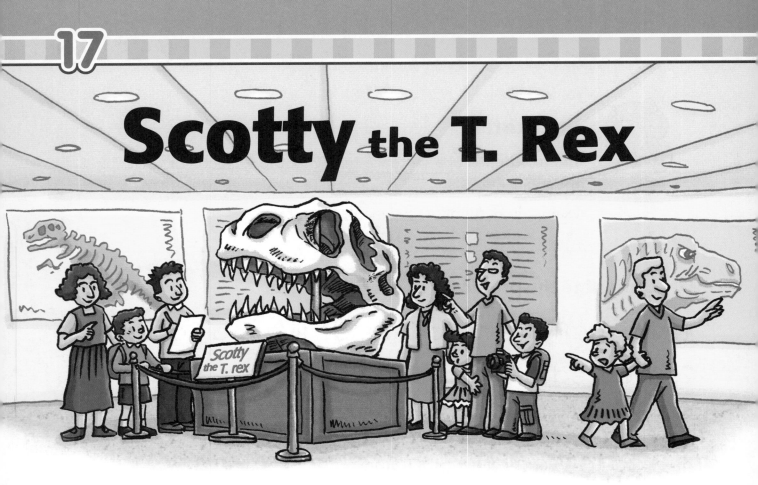

Who is Scotty the T. rex? He is one of the world's most complete dinosaurs, and he lives in a little town called Eastend, Saskatchewan!

No, Scotty is not alive. He is a dinosaur skeleton. But what makes Scotty so special is that his bones are still together in one place. Dinosaurs died millions of years ago, so we usually find dinosaur bones all jumbled up. We do not often find dinosaur bones together as a skeleton. Scotty's skeleton is only one of 12 such discoveries in the world.

Scotty's first bones were discovered by a schoolteacher from Eastend in 1991. Some scientists came to check out where they were found, and they discovered that it was the skeleton of a Tyrannosaurus rex! Now you can see Scotty for yourself at the T. rex Discovery Centre in Eastend.

A.   Read the story. Check ✔ the main idea of each paragraph.

Paragraph One

| A | Scotty the T. rex is one of the world's most complete dinosaurs. |

| B | There are dinosaurs in Eastend, Saskatchewan. |

Paragraph Two

| A | Dinosaur bones are usually found jumbled up. |

| B | Scotty is a dinosaur skeleton. |

Paragraph Three

| A | The schoolteacher who found Scotty's bones was a scientist. |

| B | Scotty's bones were discovered in 1991 and scientists found out that they belonged to a T. rex. |

Punctuation

All sentences end with punctuation marks.

A telling sentence or an imperative sentence ends with a ".". An asking sentence ends with a "?". A surprising sentence ends with an "!".

B. Put the correct punctuation mark at the end of each sentence.

1. Where are Scotty's bones

2. They're just around the corner

3. What an awesome dinosaur skull

4. When was it discovered

5. It was found more than 20 years ago

6. Take a picture of it

7. Can you e-mail the picture to me

8. Give me your e-mail address

9. That's great

Commas

Commas can be used to separate items in a list.

Example: Spain, Italy, and France are all country names.

C. Read the sentences. Add commas where needed.

1. You can go to Marineland in these months: July August and September.

2. We fed fish deer and killer whales in Marineland.

3. Dolphins walruses and sea lions performed in the shows.

4. We had salad steak cheesecake and tea for dinner.

5. You need these to make the drink: soda coconut milk and pineapple juice.

6. There are four main characters in the story. They are Celia Lester Robert and Tommy.

7. Chips lollipops ice cream and chocolate are all my favourite treats.

My Little Sister's Challenge

My little sister has a big challenge right now. She is two-and-a-half years old. My mom says it is time for her to start using the toilet.

I want to help my sister say goodbye to her diapers. Sometimes I ask her if she wants to go to the toilet. I go with her, and I show her how to do it! She watches me, but then she gets scared and uses her diaper.

★　★　★

Hey, guess what! Today my sister said she wanted to use the toilet. My mom and I took her to the washroom and helped her sit on the toilet. We waited. Nothing happened. Then I had an idea. I turned on the tap. It made a sound of running water. My sister looked at me and smiled. Then she did it!

My mom and I cheered and clapped for my sister. My sister was very proud. And we are very proud of her. Goodbye diapers!

A. Read the meanings and unscramble the letters. Write the words in the boxes.

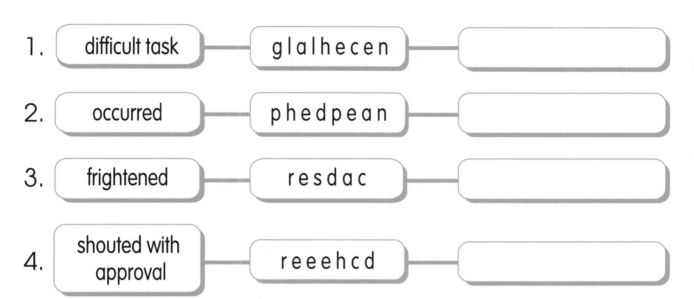

1. difficult task — g l a l h e c e n —

2. occurred — p h e d p e a n —

3. frightened — r e s d a c —

4. shouted with approval — r e e e h c d —

B. Give short answers to the questions.

1. How old is the writer's sister?

_____

2. What was the challenge for the writer's sister?

_____

3. How did the writer's sister feel when the writer showed her how to use the toilet?

_____

4. How did the writer's sister feel the first time she had used the toilet?

_____

Subject Pronouns

A pronoun replaces a noun. A **subject pronoun** acts as the subject in a sentence.

"I", "you", "we", "they", "he", "she", and "it" are subject pronouns.

Example: My brother likes sports. <u>He</u> is good at playing basketball.

C. Draw lines to match the nouns with the subject pronouns.

we •

they •

he •

she •

it •

• **A** my mom

• **B** the challenge

• **C** my sister and I

• **D** the actor

• **E** the pets

D. Fill in the blanks with the correct subject pronouns.

1. _____ am proud of my sister.

2. My dad is a chef. _____ loves cooking.

3. Can _____ lend me your ruler?

4. Kim and Liz are neighbours. _____ go to the same school too.

Object Pronouns

An **object pronoun** acts as an object that receives the action of the verb in a sentence.

"Me", "you", "us", "them", "him", "her", and "it" are object pronouns.

Example: I will give <u>you</u> a call tonight.

E. **Replace the underlined words with the correct object pronouns.**

1. Daddy bought something for <u>my sister and me</u>. _____

2. He gave <u>I</u> a box of crayons. _____

3. He said that I could use <u>the crayons</u> to draw pictures for him. _____

4. He bought a teddy bear for <u>my sister</u>. _____

5. She giggled when she saw <u>the teddy bear</u>. _____

6. I gave <u>Dad</u> a big hug. _____

7. I said "thank <u>him</u>" to my dad. _____

Canada's
Great Polar Bear Swim

Every year, on New Year's Day, people jump into the icy cold waters of English Bay, Vancouver, for a swim. It is time for the Polar Bear Swim!

Many swimming clubs all over the world host events like this. It is a fun and interesting way to celebrate the new year. But only in northern countries like Canada will the water be cold. This is why it is called a Polar Bear Swim.

The Vancouver Polar Bear Swim Club is one of the largest and oldest Polar Bear clubs in the world. Their first Polar Bear Swim was held in 1920. At that time, only ten swimmers dared to enter the event.

Now, more than 2000 brave Polar Bear swimmers run and jump into the freezing water each year. After that, everyone will go to a party to celebrate the beginning of a new year.

A. Fill in the blanks with words from the passage.

1. The Polar Bear Swim is a fun way to _____ the new year.

2. The water is cold in _____ countries.

3. There were ten _____ in the first Polar Bear Swim.

4. A _____ will be held after the swim.

B. Read the passage and answer the questions.

1. When is the Polar Bear Swim held every year?

   _____

2. Where is the event held in Vancouver?

   _____

3. When was the first swim held by the Vancouver Polar Bear Swim Club?

   _____

4. How many swimmers enter the event now?

   _____

Present Tense Verbs

A verb tells what someone or something does. A **present tense verb** tells about someone's habit or what happens now. Add "s/es" to the base form of the verb to tell about one person or thing, except "I" and "you". Use the base form for all other subjects.

Examples: Christine <u>goes</u> to Riverdale School.
Her brothers <u>go</u> to North Park School.

C. Circle the "s/es" form of the given verbs in the word search.

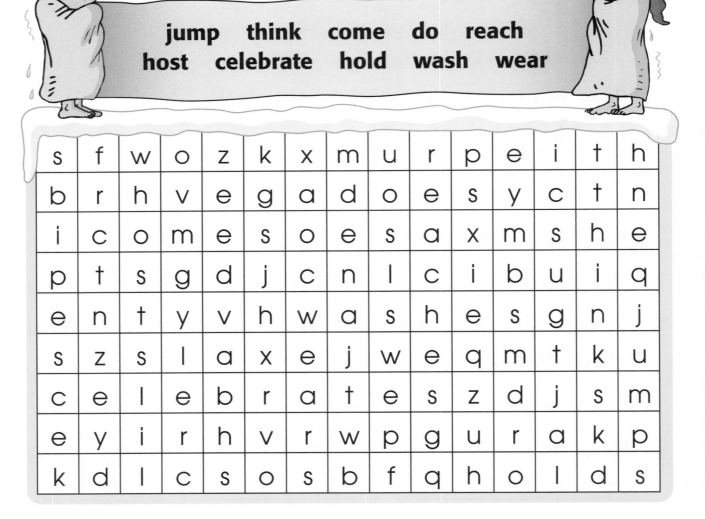

jump   think   come   do   reach
host   celebrate   hold   wash   wear

s	f	w	o	z	k	x	m	u	r	p	e	i	t	h
b	r	h	v	e	g	a	d	o	e	s	y	c	t	n
i	c	o	m	e	s	o	e	s	a	x	m	s	h	e
p	t	s	g	d	j	c	n	l	c	i	b	u	i	q
e	n	t	y	v	h	w	a	s	h	e	s	g	n	j
s	z	s	l	a	x	e	j	w	e	q	m	t	k	u
c	e	l	e	b	r	a	t	e	s	z	d	j	s	m
e	y	i	r	h	v	r	w	p	g	u	r	a	k	p
k	d	l	c	s	o	s	b	f	q	h	o	l	d	s

D. Check ✔ if the underlined verbs are correct. Rewrite the sentences with the wrong verbs.

1. The club <u>organize</u> the event.

   _____

2. Many members <u>joins</u> the Polar Bear Swim.

   _____

3. They <u>swim</u> in the freezing water.

   _____

4. I <u>wants</u> to join the swim this year.

   _____

5. My friend Celia <u>swim</u> every day.

   _____

6. You <u>need</u> to pay for the swimming course.

   _____

Why the Sea Is Salty
A Folktale from the Philippines

A long time ago, the sea tasted like rain. There was a friendly giant who kept salt in his cave across the sea. People would cross the sea and ask for salt to make their food taste better.

One day there was a storm. The people could not go out to the sea for a long time. They ran out of salt. The kind giant stretched his leg across the sea so that the people could walk to his cave. But the giant's foot landed on an anthill. Big, red ants started biting the giant's leg.

The people filled their bags with salt and began to return home. The ants bit the giant's leg again. The giant cried out and put his sore leg into the sea. The ants fell in the water, and so did the people and the bags of salt. The giant saved the people, but the salt melted in the water. From that day on, the sea was salty.

A. Read the story. Colour the correct answers.

1. The sea tasted like ___ a long time ago.

A   B   C

2. The giant kept salt in his ___ .

A   B   C

3. The people could not go out to the sea because there was a ___ .

A   B   C

4. The ___ bit the giant's leg.

 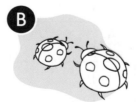 

A   B   C

5. The people filled their bags with ___ .

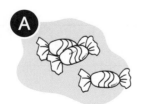  

A   B   C

Past Tense Verbs

A **past tense verb** tells about something that happened in the past.

For most verbs, add "d/ed" to the base form to change them to the past form.

Some past tense verbs are formed by repeating the last letter before adding "ed".

Examples: use → used   walk → walked   pat → patted

B. Complete the crossword puzzle with the past form of the clue words.

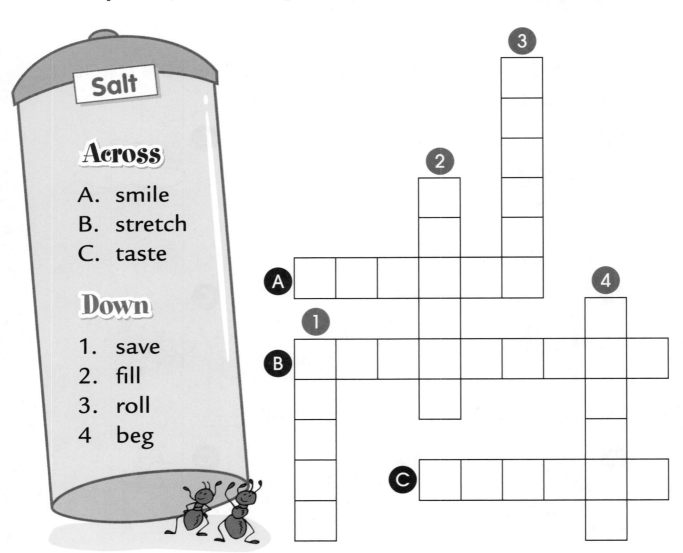

Across

A. smile
B. stretch
C. taste

Down

1. save
2. fill
3. roll
4 beg

C. Circle the correct words to complete the sentences.

1. The giant liveed / lived by the sea.

2. It rained / rainned heavily.

3. The sea water rushed / rushhed to the shore.

4. The people stoped / stopped going out to the sea.

5. The giant helped / helpped the people.

D. Rewrite the paragraph below using the simple past tense.

Mom cooks a large pot of soup. She chops some potatoes and carrots and adds them to the soup. After about an hour, she sprinkles some salt in the soup. Then she ladles the soup into bowls. We all enjoy the soup.

Mom cooked a large pot of soup last night. _____

_____

_____

_____

_____

My Grandma's Special Hobby

My grandma has a special hobby. She loves to knit. When I was born, she knitted me all my baby clothes. When I grew older, she knitted me sweaters and scarves.

One day, my grandma said she was going to start knitting for other people too. Now she knits tiny caps for babies in hospital. Grandma told me that sometimes babies are born too early. These early bird babies are tiny.

Grandma uses special wool for these little caps. She shows me some of the little caps she made. They are so tiny! It makes me feel sad to think about the small babies.

Grandma tells me not to be sad. She says that these babies have a fighting spirit. They stay in hospital for many weeks or even months. They are much bigger and healthier when they go home.

I think Grandma is doing a great job!

A. Check ✔ if the sentences are true.

1. Knitting is Grandma's hobby.

2. Grandma knitted sweaters and scarves for the writer.

3. Grandma also knitted caps and mittens for babies.

4. Babies that are born too early are tiny.

5. The writer was sad about the small babies.

6. Grandma thinks that the babies like fighting.

B. Draw a picture to show your hobby. Write a sentence about it.

My Hobby

_____

Am, Is, and Are (1)

"**Am**", "**is**", or "**are**" tells what someone or something is.

Use "am" with "I".
Use "is" to tell about one person, animal, place, or thing.
Use "are" with "you" and to tell about more than one person, animal, place, or thing.

Examples: I <u>am</u> eager to know the result.
Rachel <u>is</u> the team leader.
You <u>are</u> my best friend.

C. Colour the boxes with the correct words for the sentences.

1. Grandma ⏐ am ⏐ is ⏐ are ⏐ kind to everyone.

2. Knitting ⏐ am ⏐ is ⏐ are ⏐ her hobby.

3. The caps she knitted ⏐ am ⏐ is ⏐ are ⏐ tiny.

4. They ⏐ am ⏐ is ⏐ are ⏐ for early born babies in hospital.

5. The hospital ⏐ am ⏐ is ⏐ are ⏐ near our home.

6. I ⏐ am ⏐ is ⏐ are ⏐ proud of Grandma.

7. Our cat ⏐ am ⏐ is ⏐ are ⏐ always by her side when she knits.

Am, Is, and Are (2)

"Am", "is", or "are" can be used with the "ing" form of a verb to tell what someone or something is doing.

Examples: I <u>am studying</u> for the test.
Mom <u>is cooking</u> in the kitchen.
The kittens <u>are sleeping</u>.

D. Fill in the blanks with "am", "is", or "are" and the "ing" form of the correct verbs.

play   fish   show   do   shut   run   learn   make

1. Sarah _____ her classmates her sticker collection.

2. I _____ a model plane.

3. The children _____ a game of soccer.

4. You _____ a great job.

5. Josh and Derek _____ in a boat.

6. Linda and I _____ English.

7. The computer _____ down.

8. The dog _____ after the ball.

Fluffy the Wonder Dog

Fluffy was a special dog. One day, Fluffy was playing with his friend Toby Green. After a while, Toby began to play on the slide. Fluffy wanted to play on the slide too. He climbed up the ladder and then slid down the slide! Toby asked Fluffy to do it again but Fluffy did not want to. He did it once, and that was fine for him.

The next day, Mr. Green sent Fluffy outside to get the morning newspaper. After a while, Mr. Green opened the door for Fluffy, but there was no newspaper in Fluffy's mouth! Mr. Green told Fluffy again to get the paper. Fluffy looked sad, but he went out anyway. When he came back, he had a newspaper in his mouth.

Just then, Mrs. Green came by. She asked why Fluffy had a newspaper. Mr. Green said he told Fluffy to get it. Mrs. Green laughed. She reminded Mr. Green that it was Sunday...and that there was no morning newspaper on Sundays!

A. **Help Fluffy get the newspaper. Unscramble the letters and write the words.**

1. c p s l a e i

   _____

2. l i w e h

   _____

3. d s i e l

   _____

4. r o n i m g n

   _____

5. l r e d a d

   _____

6. r a p p e

   _____

7. b i e c d l m

   _____

8. t o u m h

   _____

9. g a e d l u h

   _____

10. e d e d m i r n

    _____

Was and Were (1)

"**Was**" or "**were**" tells about someone or something in the past.

Use "was" to tell about one person, animal, place, or thing.
Use "were" with "you" and to tell about more than one person, animal, place, or thing.

Examples: The trip to P.E.I. last summer <u>was</u> wonderful.
The lobsters there <u>were</u> huge.

B. Fill in the blanks with "was" or "were".

1. My dog Penny _____ special.

2. He _____ small and cute but his barks _____ loud.

3. He _____ able to dance to the music too.

4. I _____ amazed to see him dance.

5. My dad made a doghouse for him. It _____ his favourite spot.

6. Cookies _____ his favourite treats.

7. We _____ all happy to have him in our family.

Was and Were (2)

"Was" or "were" can be used with the "ing" form of a verb to tell what someone or something was doing at a past time.

Examples: Jackie <u>was walking</u> his dog when he met Roy.
We <u>were playing</u> games when the lights went out.

C. Check ✔ if the underlined words are correct. Correct the wrong words and write them in the 🐱 .

1. Mr. and Mrs. Howell <u>was</u> watching TV when their children came home.

2. I was <u>have</u> lunch with Meg at noon yesterday.

3. Kitty <u>was</u> doing show-and-tell when the bell rang.

4. My sister and I were <u>cycle</u> when we met Jenny.

5. The kitten was drinking milk while the puppies <u>were</u> eating pet food.

6. The melted chocolate <u>were</u> dripping out from a spout.

A New Student in Class

Date: _____

Dear Diary,

Today was a happy day at school. A new girl named Emi came to my class. After lunch, she showed us her skipping rope. It was a nice, pink skipping rope. I was jealous. My skipping rope is old. It is not pink. I like pink.

Emi asked us to play with her. I said no. But all my friends said yes. I was angry at my best friend. She was playing with Emi and not me!

I sat alone on the swing. I felt sad and lonely.

Soon, my friend came over to me. She asked me to play with everyone. I felt ashamed. I wanted to play. I wanted to be friends with Emi.

I said yes. Everyone was glad I came to play. Emi is a good skipper. We will all be good friends.

I was very happy after that.

A. **Unscramble the letters and write the words that show how the writer felt.**

1. d s a _____

2. r a g y n _____

3. e s l o j a u _____

4. y p h p a _____

5. e o y l l n _____

6. a m h e a d s _____

B. **Check ✔ if the sentences are true.**

1. The new classmate is a girl. ☐

2. The writer has a pink skipping rope. ☐

3. The new classmate sat on the swing alone. ☐

4. The other students did not want the writer to join them. ☐

5. Emi skips well. ☐

Adjectives

An **adjective** describes a noun. It tells how someone or something looks or feels. Colour words, number words, and shapes are all adjectives.

Example: The <u>two</u> <u>oval</u> dishes are <u>blue</u>.

C. Circle the adjectives. Then complete the crossword puzzle with the circled words.

old
nice
shelf
good
share
three
violet
round
twelve
heavily
scared
beside
square

D. **Choose an adjective from (C) to describe each noun. Draw a picture to go with it.**

_____ clock   _____ flowers

E. **Fill in the blanks with the given adjectives.**

crazy   delicious   round   red   favourite   five

1. Strawberries are _____ in colour.

2. They taste _____ with whipped cream.

3. There are only _____ strawberries left.

4. Susanne is _____ about all kinds of berries.

5. Her _____ berries are blueberries.

6. She likes eating them in a _____ salad bowl.

A New Game

Grandpa gave me a small bag. Inside, there was a small rubber ball and 15 small metal things. They each had six spikes. Grandpa called them "jacks".

Grandpa gathered all the jacks in one hand and then let them go onto the floor. They scattered around a little bit. Then Grandpa gently tossed the ball into the air. While the ball was in the air, Grandpa grabbed one jack. Then, with the same hand, he caught the ball after it bounced once.

Then Grandpa and I repeated the game, but this time we had to pick up two jacks at a time. When the jacks were all taken, we played again. This time we had to pick up three jacks at a time, and then four and then five and then six!

It was a lot of fun. Grandpa said he had never picked up more than eight jacks at once. But his friend could pick up 11! I like this game.

A.   Put the sentences in order. Write 1 to 6.

◯ Pick up one jack on the floor.

◯ Toss the ball into the air.

◯ Let the ball bounce once.

◯ Scatter the jacks onto the floor.

◯ Repeat, each time picking up one more jack.

◯ Catch the ball with the same hand.

B.   Colour Y if the sentence is true.   Colour N if it is not.

1. The game is played with a small ball and 15 jacks.   Y | N

2. There are six spikes on each jack.   Y | N

3. Grandpa grabbed a jack with one hand and caught the ball with the other hand.   Y | N

4. Grandpa could pick up 11 jacks at one go.   Y | N

5. The writer found the game boring.   Y | N

Prepositions (1)

Some **prepositions** tell where people, animals, and things are.

"In", "on", "behind", "beside", "between", "under", and "over" are some of them.

Example: We kept our fish <u>in</u> a fishbowl.

C. Read and complete the picture.

- Draw a cat sleeping <u>on</u> the bench.
- Draw a ball <u>beside</u> the cat.
- Draw a girl with a basket <u>behind</u> the bench.
- Draw six apples <u>in</u> the basket.
- Draw three flowers <u>under</u> the bench.
- Draw a bird flying <u>over</u> the rock.
- Draw a squirrel <u>between</u> the rock and the bench.
- Colour your picture.

Prepositions (2)

Some prepositions are used with other words to tell when someone does something or when something happens.

Use "at" with times and festivals; use "on" with days; use "in" with months, years, and seasons.

Examples: <u>at</u> two o'clock   <u>on</u> Monday   <u>in</u> June

D. Draw lines to match the words with the prepositions.

at •

on •

in •

• **A** summer

• **B** Saturday

• **C** August

• **D** Christmas

• **E** eight thirty

• **F** 2015

E. Write sentences with prepositions and the given words.

1. Easter

_____

2. four o'clock yesterday

_____

I Want to Be a...

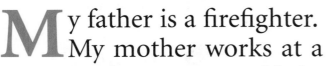

My father is a firefighter. My mother works at a supermarket. My grandfather works at the City Hall. My grandmother works in a daycare centre. My neighbour is a cab driver.

I am not sure what I want to be. I like animals, so maybe I will work in a zoo or be a vet. I like food, so maybe I will be a waitress or a chef. I like dressing up, so maybe I will be a clothes designer or a photographer or a hair stylist. Maybe I will be a teacher or a doctor or a dancer!

My grandmother told me that if I study hard, I will have more choices about what I want to be when I grow up. She also says that, right now, I should learn more things. Later, I will know what I am good at and I can decide what I want to do. I think this is a good idea.

A. Check ✔ the pictures that show what the writer wants to be.

1.

2.

3.

4.

5.

6.

7.

8.

B. Draw a picture to show what you want to be when you grow up. Write a sentence to go with it.

_____

_____

Connecting Words

Connecting words are used to join words or sentences.

"And" is used to join items in a list to show addition.
"Or" is used to join options to show choices.
"But" is used to join two contrasting ideas.

Examples: May, Sarah, <u>and</u> Jim are my best friends.
For dessert, you can have mango mousse <u>or</u> sundae.
Dad loves fishing <u>but</u> I find it boring.

C. Draw a ☺ if the connecting word in each sentence is correct. Draw a ☹ if it is wrong.

1. I want to be a chef, a designer, or a dancer.

2. Do you want to be a doctor or work in a hospital?

3. My father works long hours but he likes his job.

4. I have to study hard and learn more at school.

5. My mom only has one day off in a week. It is Saturday and Sunday.

D. **Add "and", "or", or "but". Use a $\wedge$ to show where you add it in the sentence.**

1. I need bread, ham, cheese to make the sandwich.

2. You can pick only one, the one with the bunny the one with the bear.

3. We can keep this ending write a new ending to our play.

4. The play was great the ending was too sad.

E. **Join the two sentences with "and", "or", or "but".**

1. I don't like sweet things. This dessert is delicious.

   _____

   _____

2. My family is going on a trip. Sally is joining us.

   _____

   _____

3. We can meet at the theatre. I can pick you up.

   _____

   _____

When Grandma Was a Girl Like Me

Today Grandma gave me a new piggy bank and some paints! I had fun painting my piggy bank. Grandma gave me a toonie to put in my piggy bank too.

Then Grandma told me a story about herself when she was my age. One day, she went to a country fair with her parents. Her father gave her a dollar.

He said, "You can buy some candy or you can buy a baby chick. You can take the chick home and feed it. It will grow big and lay eggs. Then you can sell the eggs. You will have more chickens, too, and they will lay eggs. Someday you will have more than one dollar."

My grandmother looked at the candy. Then she looked up at her father and said, "I will buy a baby chick."

When they got home, her father showed her how to take care of the chick. Then he gave her a big kiss – and a candy from his pocket.

A. **Read, draw, and write.**

- Draw some coins in the piggy bank.
- Draw the thing you want to buy with the money next to the piggy bank.
- Write a sentence about the thing you want to buy.
- Colour the picture.

_____

B. **Check ✔ if the sentences are true.**

1. Grandma's father gave her a toonie.   ____

2. Grandma could buy some candy or a chick.   ____

3. The chick would grow big and lay eggs.   ____

4. Grandma's father was not happy with Grandma's decision.   ____

5. Grandma's father gave her a candy.   ____

Synonyms and Antonyms

Synonyms are words that have similar meanings.

Examples: young – little

Antonyms are words that have opposite meanings.

Examples: young – old

C. Write the words in the correct places.

> dawn   small   light   smart
> cheerful   arrive   fast   damp

🥚 Synonym 🐥

1. clever _____

2. wet _____

3. daybreak _____

4. happy _____

🥚 Antonym 🐥

5. big _____

6. slow _____

7. leave _____

8. heavy _____

D. Find the synonym and antonym of each word in the word search. Colour the synonym yellow and the antonym pink.

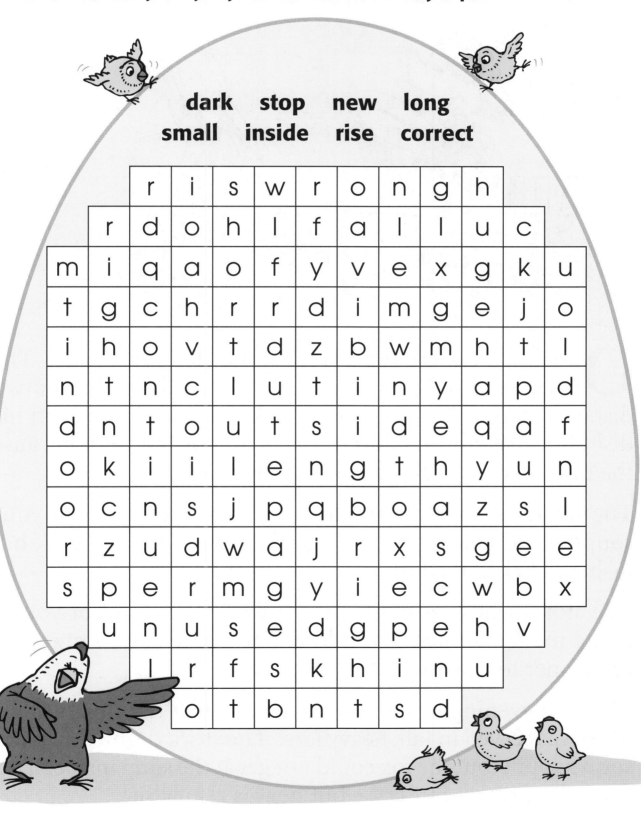

dark   stop   new   long
small   inside   rise   correct

r	i	s	w	r	o	n	g	h	
r	d	o	h	l	f	a	l	l	u	c
m	i	q	a	o	f	y	v	e	x	g	k	u
t	g	c	h	r	r	d	i	m	g	e	j	o
i	h	o	v	t	d	z	b	w	m	h	t	l
n	t	n	c	l	u	t	i	n	y	a	p	d
d	n	t	o	u	t	s	i	d	e	q	a	f
o	k	i	i	l	e	n	g	t	h	y	u	n
o	c	n	s	j	p	q	b	o	a	z	s	l
r	z	u	d	w	a	j	r	x	s	g	e	e
s	p	e	r	m	g	y	i	e	c	w	b	x
u	n	u	s	e	d	g	p	e	h	v
l	r	f	s	k	h	i	n	u
o	t	b	n	t	s	d

The **Fox** and the **Stork**

One day, a fox invited a stork to his den for dinner. The stork sat down at the table, and the fox brought out two dishes of soup. The fox quickly licked up all the soup in his dish, but the stork could not drink any of the soup because the dish was too shallow for her long beak.

The fox licked his lips and asked, "Why didn't you eat your soup?" And before the stork could answer, the fox took her dish and licked it all up.

The stork, who was polite, said only, "It was kind of you to invite me for dinner. I would like to invite you to my place for dinner tomorrow."

The next evening, when the fox sat down at the stork's table, soup was served in tall, heavy jars. The stork drank down her soup happily, but the fox could not get at the soup inside. This time, the fox was hungry – but he was also wiser.

A.   Put the sentences in order. Write 1 to 6.

The stork invited the fox for dinner.

The fox invited the stork to his den.

The stork finished her soup.

The fox finished the stork's soup.

The fox became wiser.

The stork could not drink the dish of soup.

B.   Fill in the blanks with words from the story.

1. The fox lived in a _____ .

2. He _____ the stork for dinner.

3. He served the soup in _____ dishes.

4. He _____ up all his soup.

5. The stork could not drink the soup because of her long _____ .

6. When the fox had dinner at the stork's place, soup was served in tall, heavy _____ .

Not (1)

The word "**not**" can be added to a sentence to form the negative.

Use "am/is/are not" to tell about something in the present. Use "am/is/are not" and the "ing" form of a verb to tell about what is not going on.

Examples: We <u>are not</u> upset.
It <u>is not raining</u>.

C. Use a ∧ **to add "not" in the correct places to form negative sentences.**

1. The fox is adding salt to the soup.

2. The soup is boiling.

3. It is very hot.

4. The bowls are big.

5. They are made of clay.

6. I am hungry.

7. I am drinking the soup.

8. They are washing the dishes.

Not (2)

We can also use the negative to talk about the present by adding "does not" before the base form of the verb for a singular subject except "I" and "you".

For a plural subject, "I", and "you", add "do not" before the base form.

Examples: The bus <u>does not stop</u> here.
Cats <u>do not swim</u>.

D.   Fill in the blanks by changing the given verbs to negative.

1. Richard _____ (mind) sharing his toys with me.

2. Florence _____ (have) any purple dresses.

3. I _____ (go) to Northville School.

4. We _____ (ride) our bikes on the road.

5. The weather is nice. You _____ (need) to take the umbrella with you.

6. The clever squirrel _____ (hide) the acorns in our backyard.

Johnny Appleseed

Have you ever heard of the story of Johnny Appleseed? Johnny Appleseed lived in the United States more than 200 years ago. His real name was John Chapman.

John Chapman loved planting trees. By the time he was 25 years old, he had already planted many apple trees in what is now New York State and Pennsylvania. In the 1800s, John went to the land south of the Great Lakes and west of the Ohio River. He cleared small squares of land in the wilderness and planted rows of trees. Soon, John became known as the Apple Tree Man, or Johnny Appleseed.

Johnny had no family. He was a kind and gentle man. He was a friend to the Native Americans living in the area, as well as the settlers coming in. He was a great storyteller, and children loved him very much.

John Chapman died in 1845, but many of his apple trees are still standing.

A. Read the sentences. Circle the answers in the word search.

1. The real name of Johnny Appleseed was ___ .

2. He lived in the ___ .

3. He grew ___ in New York State.

4. Later, he went to the land west of the ___ .

5. He was kind and ___ .

6. He and the Native Americans were ___ .

7. Children loved him because he was a great ___ .

l	h	a	v	j	r	m			
e	p	d	O	p	U	o	s	a	g	k
s	c	a	p	p	l	e		t	r	e	e	s
n	j		m	f	i	g	R	a		n	C	j
b	s	t	o	r	y	t	e	l	l	e	r	d
t	g	O	h	i	o		R	i	v	e	r	n
U	n	i	t	e	d		S	t	a	t	e	s
w	J	o	h	n		C	h	a	p	m	a	n
o	l	U	p	d	a	q	O	e	j	c	i	f
k	b	h	s	f	g	e	n	t	l	e		

Sequencing

Sentences should be put in a logical order so that people can follow the idea.

B. Put the sentences in order. Write the letters.

1. **A** We all enjoy eating the pies.

   B Every summer, many apples grow in the tree.

   C Then Mom bakes apple pies with them.

   D Dad picks the big, red apples.

   E We have an apple tree in our backyard.

2. **A** They laughed when they saw the funny characters.

   B Valerie and her sister went to the theatre.

   C The movie started.

   D They had a great time.

   E They bought some popcorn.

C. **Put the pictures in order by writing the letters in the** 🐾 **. Then write sentences about them.**

1. _____

2. _____

3. _____

4. _____

5. _____

6. _____

SOCIAL STUDIES

My Family

Each of us is part of a family. Families come in all shapes and sizes.

A. Draw or paste a photo of your family below. Then write who each family member is.

mom

dad

brother

sister

My Family

uncle

aunt

cousin

grandpa

grandma

B. Ask a family member about special events that have happened. Write them down. Then complete your family timeline.

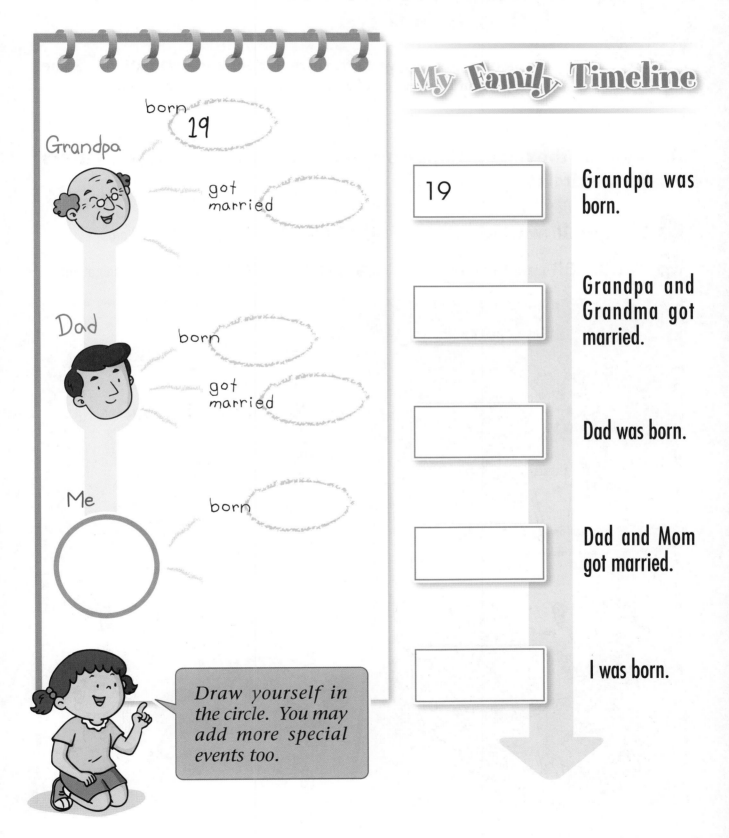

Different Traditions and Celebrations

Different cultures have different traditions and celebrations. Some special traditions and celebrations are important to a family.

A. Identify the celebrations from different cultures. Write the letters in the circles.

A **Eid ul-Fitr** (Muslim holiday)

B **Powwow** (Indigenous celebration)

C **Hanukkah** (Jewish holiday)

D **Lunar New Year** (Chinese celebration)

B. **Think of a family celebration that is important to you. Write the name of the celebration and add three more lines to complete the song.**

My Family Celebration

We celebrate

What is passed along.

We celebrate

Our traditions through our song.

your celebration

Is when we

Our Powwow

Is when we come together.

A summer gathering

to meet each other.

Traditional Foods

Heritage is celebrations and special practices passed down in our families. Traditions have been passed down from parents to children through the years.

A. The children are introducing their traditional foods. Name their traditional foods and write where they come from.

> *My grandpa likes to make **turnip cake** with me for Chinese New Year because it is a special traditional food in **China**.*

> *My nonna shows me how to make **gnocchi** for her tasty tomato sauce. She got the recipe from her grandma in **Italy**.*

> *I like to help my mom make **oliebollen**. These sweet doughnuts from **the Netherlands** are my favourite treats!*

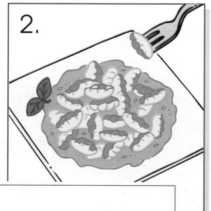

Traditional Foods

1.

_____

from

_____

2.

_____

from

_____

3.

_____

from

_____

B. **Think of a tradition that your parents or grandparents have passed down to you. Draw or paste a picture of it in the box. Then write about it.**

The Heritage Times

The tradition that has been passed down to me:

_____ by _____

1. What makes it special?

_____

2. Is it used for celebrations? If so, what does it celebrate?

_____

3. Will you pass it down to your children?

_____

Our Traditions and Celebrations

Our traditions and celebrations may be the same as or different from those of others. Traditional celebrations are usually related to rites of passage, holidays, and foods.

A. Fill in the blanks to complete the paragraph about Diwali. Then colour to light the candles.

Diwali –
The Festival of Lights

candles   five-day   November
Indian   kheer   Lights

Diwali is one of the biggest 1._____ festivals which celebrates the New Year. This festival is usually celebrated in October or 2._____ . Diwali is a 3._____ celebration. People decorate their homes with lamps and 4._____ to show the victory of light over darkness, which is why the festival is also known as the Festival of 5._____ . 6._____ , a milky rice pudding, and coconut sweets are the special foods of Diwali.

B. Read the paragraph about Hanukkah. Then check ✔ the correct picture.

A Menorah

Hanukkah is the Jewish Festival of Lights, which lasts for eight days. It usually falls in late November or December. Jewish families light candles in a menorah (a nine-branched candle holder) for the eight days of Hanukkah. During Hanukkah, families eat latkes (potato pancakes) and sufganiyot (jelly doughnuts).

C. Complete the chart using the information from (A) and (B).

Festival	Diwali	Hanukkah
Another Name		
Celebrated by		
Things People Do		
Foods People Eat		

5

Ethnic Foods and Things

In Canada, we have the freedom to keep our own traditions and follow other traditions if we like. This makes Canada an interesting place to live in.

A. **See what the children want to buy. Take them to the correct communities. Write the letters.**

B. **Look at the ethnic foods and draw two more. Choose the ethnic foods that your family eats and ask a friend about the choices of his or her family. Then record the choices in the diagram.**

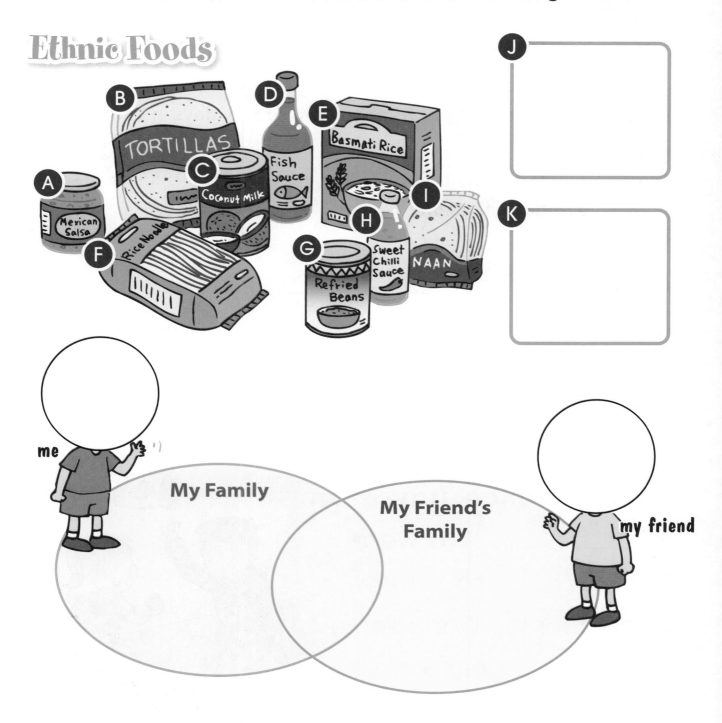

Would you like to try some ethnic foods that you have never tried before? _____

Special Days

There are special days during the year that celebrate or commemorate important events. Some events are celebrated in many countries, while others are unique to a particular country.

A. Complete the paragraphs about two special days in Canada.

flag July 1 birthday fireworks	poppies soldiers November 11

Canada Day is on 1._____ . It is the celebration of Canada's 2._____ . On this day, we have 3._____ . We also fly the Canadian 4._____ to show how much we love our country.

Remembrance Day is on 5._____ . We wear 6._____ to show respect for the Canadian 7._____ who served our country.

poppies

B. **Read how some people in Canada celebrate their traditional New Year. Then help the children choose the correct foods to get ready for the New Year. Write the letters.**

Iranian Canadians celebrate their New Year on March 21, the first day of spring. Families set the table with seven "S" items. They are:

seer (garlic)

samanu (pudding)

seeb (apple)

sonbol (flowers)

serkeh (vinegar)

sekeh (coins)

sabzeh (sprouts)

Chinese Canadians celebrate their New Year on the first day of the Lunar calendar. They usually celebrate with a feast that may include foods such as:

- boiled dumplings
- long noodles
- steamed fish

Traditional Foods

A

B

C

D

E

F

G

Changing Traditions

Cultural traditions can change as they are passed down through generations. These traditions can be celebrations, festivals, and lifestyles.

A. **Read about these traditions. Then give a reason for the change in each tradition.**

Shrove Tuesday used to be a special day when Christians used up all the milk, butter, and eggs at home to make pancakes before the fasting season of Lent. Since pancakes were eaten on Shrove Tuesday, this day was also known as Pancake Day. Today, people still celebrate Shrove Tuesday with pancakes but now they add different ingredients such as salmon, mocha syrup, and chocolate spread to make the pancakes even more flavourful.

Do you want more?

Yes, please.

A Reason for Change

_____

_____

_____

Hanukkah is a Jewish celebration in honour of the victorious battle for religious freedom. During this eight-day celebration, Jewish families place and light candles in a menorah. The menorah is usually displayed near the front window in order to remind people walking by of this great festival. Some people today prefer electric lights to candles for their menorahs.

A Reason for Change _____

_____

*Exchanging Christmas cards is a traditional activity that many people do at **Christmas**. Sending Christmas cards to friends and family is a good way of wishing them well. This tradition still lives, but more and more people like sending e-cards instead of mailing real cards.*

A Reason for Change _____

_____

Celebrating Differently

Different families have their own cultural practices to celebrate winter holidays. Some of these holiday traditions have changed over time.

A. Read about the winter celebration of some African-Canadian families. Circle the correct words and colour the flames to light the candles in order. Then write about your own winter celebration.

Kwanzaa

Kwanzaa is a seven-day celebration from December 26 to January 1 that honours the African heritage.

Things to do:

feast	gifts	candles

1. light _____

2. have a _____

3. give children

_____

Happy Kwanzaa!

2 3 4 1 5 6 7

We have a specific way of arranging and lighting the candles to celebrate Kwanzaa!

My Winter Celebration

Things I do:

_____

_____

B. **Draw on the trees to show how your grandparents, parents, and you would decorate the Christmas trees.**

Decorations for grandparents', parents', and your Christmas trees

candle

plastic bulbs

LED light

glass bulb

plastic ornament

popcorn

tinsel

paper snowflake

wooden toy

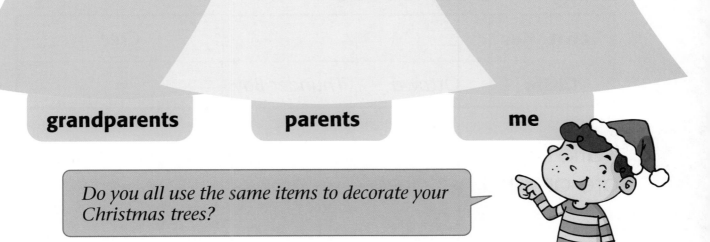

grandparents

parents

me

Do you all use the same items to decorate your Christmas trees?

9

Mapping Our Traditions

The First Nations, Métis, or Inuit peoples lived, travelled, hunted, and farmed on the land where you now live. Many still do, and today are your neighbours, classmates, or friends, or they may have been moved to other places. You can learn about their traditions and way of life, and all of the knowledge they can share with you.

A. **Look at the map of early Indigenous territories and present cities in Ontario. Then answer the questions.**

Cities on Indigenous Territories in Ontario

1. Living in the Same Area

Territories			Cree
Cities	Ottawa	Thunder Bay	

2. Katie lives in Barrie. Which Indigenous communities are around her area?

_____

B. Fill in the blanks to complete the passage.

Powwow
A Traditional Celebration of the Pic River First Nations

year

north

dance

ancestors

Canada

culture

The Indigenous Peoples were forced to move from place to place by the Europeans who moved onto their land, but some Ojibwe communities are still located in the traditional areas where their 1._____ lived.

Ojibwe peoples lived along the Pic River, on the 2._____ shore of Lake Superior. Even today, every 3._____ , the Pic River First Nations hold their traditional celebration – powwow, in which they come together and sing and 4._____ to celebrate and honour their 5._____ and community.

Today, there are powwows all across 6._____ and people from around the world are welcome to attend this celebration.

10

Our Thanksgiving Celebration

Thanksgiving is a celebration that has taken place for hundreds of years. Some of its traditions have lasted through the years, but some have changed.

A. Fill in the blanks to complete the paragraphs about how Thanksgiving was first celebrated in Canada.

| explorer | turkeys | thanks | harvest | ceremony | cranberry |

Martin Frobisher was the first person to celebrate Thanksgiving. He was an English explorer who arrived in Newfoundland in 1578. He gave 1._____ for his safe arrival to the new land we now call Canada. He did not have turkeys, but he held a special Thanksgiving 2._____ .

Samuel de Champlain was another 3._____ who celebrated Thanksgiving with a feast of thanks for a good 4._____ .
These early feasts did not necessarily have 5._____ .

Also, early settlers did not have ingredients such as butter, flour, and sugar to make the sweet 6. _____ or pumpkin pies we enjoy at today's Thanksgiving dinner.

B. Read this diary about planning for a Thanksgiving celebration many years ago. Fill in the chart and answer the question.

Food	How to Get It?

Dear Diary,

My father caught the biggest turkey we have ever seen! We finally have a bird for our Thanksgiving feast. Mother used the maple syrup made from the sap of the maple trees to make the cranberry sauce taste sweeter. Jonathan and I gathered some squash and corn too. I can hear my stomach growling now!

Yours,
Alexandra

Write one thing about your Thanksgiving meal that is different from this early celebration.

Happy Thanksgiving

Our World

Continents are the big pieces of land on Earth. There are seven continents in all. A compass rose is a symbol on a map or globe that shows directions.

A. Name the seven continents with the help of the map.

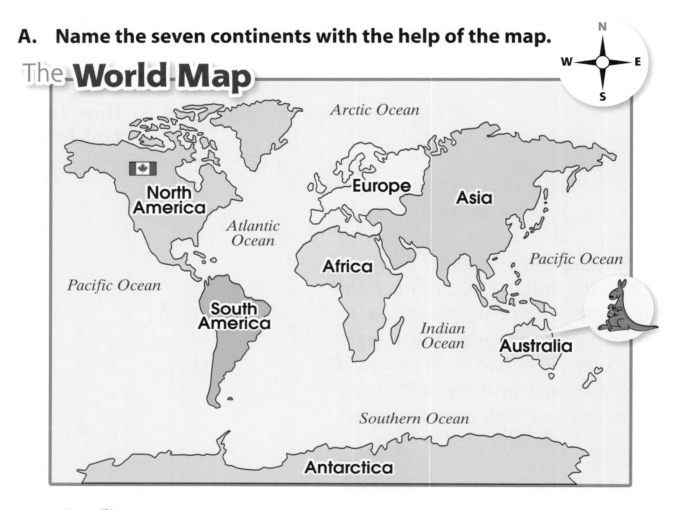

The **World Map**

Arctic Ocean

North America

Europe

Asia

Atlantic Ocean

Africa

Pacific Ocean

South America

Pacific Ocean

Indian Ocean

Australia

Southern Ocean

Antarctica

The Seven Continents

Asia

B. Match with the help of the map in (A).

Between South America and Africa is... •

Canada is in... •

Kangaroos live in... •

The largest continent is... •

- North America

- Australia

- Asia

- the Atlantic Ocean

C. Complete the compass rose. Then fill in the blanks with the help of the map in (A).

A compass rose is a symbol that shows directions: north, east, south, and west.

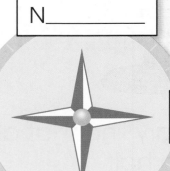

N_____

W_____

E_____

S_____

Compass Rose

1. North America is

_____ of South America.

2. Europe is _____ of North America.

The Globe

A globe is a model of the Earth. Adding lines and labelling different parts of a globe help us understand our Earth better.

A. Look at the globe. Answer the questions.

The Equator is halfway between the North Pole and the South Pole.

1. an imaginary line that divides the Earth in half _____

2. the top half of the Earth _____

3. the bottom half of the Earth _____

4. the very top of the Earth _____

5. the very bottom of the Earth _____

B. **Fill in the blanks with the given words and with the help of the globe in (A).**

 ## The Equator

water	north	land
south	snows	ice
rainforests	rain	

- receives the most sunlight
- very warm with lots of 1. _____
- home to the largest tropical 2. _____
- a country that is on the Equator: 3. _____

 ## The Northern Hemisphere

- located 4. _____ of the Equator
- has more land but less 5. _____ than the Southern Hemisphere
- a country that is in the Northern Hemisphere: 6. _____

 ## The Southern Hemisphere

- located 7. _____ of the Equator
- has less 8. _____ but more water than the Northern Hemisphere
- a country that is in the Southern Hemisphere: 9. _____

 ## The North Pole

- very cold and covered by 10. _____ everywhere
- an animal that lives in the North Pole: 11. _____

 ## The South Pole

- like a cold desert, so it rarely 12. _____
- an animal that lives in the South Pole: 13. _____

Climates of North America

North America is the third largest continent. Because of its size, places in different areas of North America have different climates.

A. **Colour the continent to complete the map showing the climates of North America. Then fill in the blanks.**

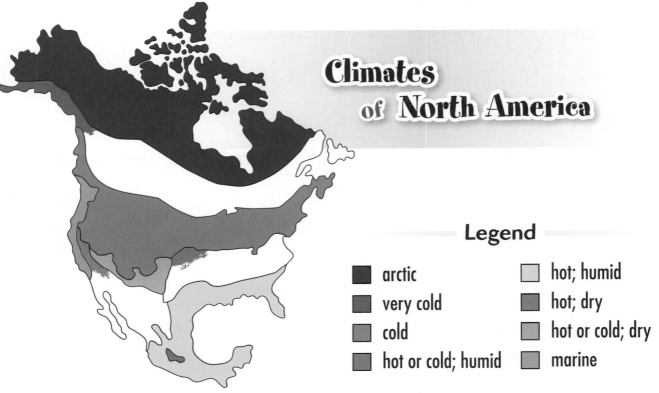

Climates of North America

Legend

- ■ arctic
- ■ very cold
- ■ cold
- ■ hot or cold; humid
- □ hot; humid
- ■ hot; dry
- ■ hot or cold; dry
- ■ marine

North America

- Canada
- United States
- Mexico

North America is made up of three main countries: _____, _____, and _____.

_____ is the warmest country and _____ is the coldest country.

258 Complete Canadian Curriculum • **Grade 2**

B. **Circle the correct words to complete the paragraph. Then identify the four seasons in Canada.**

The closer a place is to the Equator, the **colder / warmer** its climate is. The farther a place is from the Equator, the **colder / warmer** its climate is, and the more distinct the **seasons / directions** are.

Canada

coldest

warmest

coldest

Canada is far from the Equator.

Four Seasons in Canada

1. _____

2. _____

3. _____

4. _____

14

Unique Countries

There are many interesting countries in the world. Some countries, like Brazil, are homes to thousands of animal species. Other countries, like Iceland, have unusual landforms.

A. **Fill in the blanks with the given words. Then answer the question.**

Equator	Southern	warm
rainforest	south	Amazon

Map of Brazil

Equator

Amazon River

North America

South America

Brazil

- is mostly in the 1._____ Hemisphere.

- is 2._____ of Canada.

- lies on the 3._____ .

- has a 4._____ climate because most of it is south of the Equator.

- has a famous river called the 5._____ River, which runs through a 6._____ .

- is home to many animals, including about 1677 kinds of birds, 467 kinds of reptiles, 428 kinds of mammals, and 516 kinds of amphibians.

Why do you think there are so many animals in Brazil?

B. **Look at the map of Iceland. Fill in the blanks and name the landforms.**

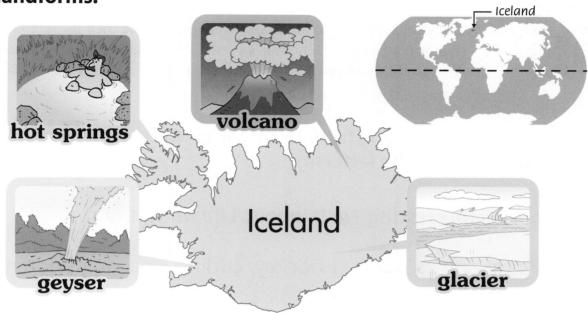

Iceland

- is in the _____ Hemisphere.

- is _____ of Canada.

- is _____ from the Equator.

- has a _____ climate.

cold
east
Northern
far

Special Landforms

1.	a spring full of natural hot water from underground
2.	a big block of ice that moves very slowly
3.	a mountain with an opening through which lava and hot gas may be ejected
4.	a big spray of hot water from an underground spring

15

Our Unique Country

Canada is a very large country. Different places have their own characteristics that affect people's way of living. People in Iqaluit, Nunavut have very different lifestyles from those living in Vancouver, British Columbia.

A. **Match the interesting facts about life in Nunavut with the correct pictures. Write the letters.**

Interesting Facts about Life in Nunavut

A Winter sports, such as hockey, curling, and dog sledding are popular.

B A sealift carries dried and canned food to the communities during the summer.

C There are no roads connecting the communities. People travel by small plane from town to town.

D Drinking water and oil for heating are shipped to the people. Every household is given limited amounts of these supplies.

B. Fill in the blanks to complete the paragraph.

Living in Vancouver, British Columbia

transportation   necessities   hiking
recreational   stores   skiing

In British Columbia, Vancouver would be the best place to live in. A large variety of 1._____ and restaurants can be found everywhere in the city, so people can get their 2._____ easily. There are many forms of 3._____ , such as BC Transit and BC Ferries, that provide frequent services for people travelling in the city. Because of Vancouver's distinct seasons, different 4._____

activities can be done in its natural environment, like 5._____ in summer and 6._____ in winter.

Vancouver, BC

Photo courtesy of Robert Lista

C. State one similarity and one difference between life in Nunavut and life in Vancouver.

Similarity: _____

Difference: _____

16

Travel around the World

Different regions in the world have their own characteristics. People travel to other parts of the world to see new things and experience different natural environments.

A. **Look at the pictures the children took on their trips. Match each country with the correct description.**

1. _____ : There are lots of Buddhist temples. Most people there are Buddhists.

2. _____ : It is a bear native to Sichuan. This lovely animal is picky. It eats only bamboo.

3. _____ : It provides shelter, clothing, food, and water for people and animals. Its fruits are full of vitamin C.

4. _____ : Surrounded by water, this place has a lot of seafood. People like to make sushi with it or eat it raw.

B. The children took pictures of beautiful natural scenery. Circle the correct words. Then put the animals in the correct environments. Write the letters.

A scorpion
B gorilla
C cheetah
D toucan
E camel
F elephant

Savannah in Africa

- a large **grassland / ocean**
- lots of different **trees / fish**
- animals **graze / swim** in it

Rainforest in South America

- gets lots of **rain / snow**
- a very big **mountain / forest**
- lots of **wildlife / wildfire**

Desert in the United States

- gets very little **rain / sun**
- has lots of **snow / sand**
- few animals and **peas / plants**

17

Our Basic Needs

We all have to meet our basic needs. Some of these needs are water, food, shelter, and transportation. People around the world have different ways of meeting their needs.

A. **Fill in the chart to compare the basic needs of the Inuit and yourself. You may use the suggested ideas or write your own.**

Water
- from taps
- from water trucks
- from water bottles

Food
- from grocery stores
- by hunting
- by fishing

Shelter
- apartment
- igloo
- house

Transportation
- small boats
- buses
- walking

Basic Needs	The Inuit	Yourself
Water		
Food		
Shelter		
Transportation		

B. Fill in the blanks to show how people living in different places get around. Then write where the people are.

subway

scooter

mule

U.S.A.

Taiwan

France

> It is very rocky here, so I ride a _____ to travel along the narrow paths.

1.

Colorado, U._____

> I take the _____ to work because it is the fastest way to get around the city.

2.

Sortie

Paris,

F_____

3.

Taipei,

T_____

> I ride my _____ to work. It is easier to get around.

18

Living around the World

No matter where we are, we all have the same basic needs: shelter, clothing, and food. But all these are met differently depending on where we live.

A. **Read the riddle about each home and match it with the correct picture. Write the letters.**

A

I am moved to a new place

When the grass is gone.

White cloth, wool, and hair

On two poles make me strong.

B

I stand on the water, made from

Wood of mangrove trees.

For the people who live inside,

The fish are easy to see.

C

Rows of painted bricks

Make my walls last.

My countless wood frames

Hold my windows fast.

Our Homes

Rheinland-Pfalz, Germany

South Gobi Desert, Mongolia

Sabah, Malaysia

B. **Fill in the blanks to see how people around the world get their food.**

seals   meat   bakery   milk   fish   food   rice

1.

Hello! My name is Bataar. I live in rural Mongolia. Our family's animals give us _____ and _____ . When the grass here is all eaten up by our animals, we'll move to a new place where there's more grass.

2. Akycha lives in Canada's Arctic. He and his father hunt _____ , like their ancestors. Groceries are very expensive where they live, so they use seal for more than just _____ .

3. Jacques lives in France. His favourite food is pastries from the _____ down the street.

4. Annisa lives in a village in the tropical hills of Indonesia. Her family grows _____ , which is their main food, and they catch _____ in the river nearby.

19

Clothes and Homes

The clothes people wear and the homes they live in are unique to each place. These clothes and houses provide people with the best protection from the climate of that particular place.

A. Look at the people in their traditional clothes from around the world. Write where they live.

Delhi, India

Nunavut, Canada

Nairobi, Kenya

Lima, Peru

I love the beautiful colours of our saris. The fabric of this sari keeps me cool in the hot weather.

1.

It can be cold in the mountains of South America, so I wear a shawl.

2.

Our clothing has been the same for many years. This covering protects me from the heat.

3.

My clothes keep me warm in freezing temperatures all year round.

4.

B. **Write the building material for each house. Read about the weather in different cities. Then match each house with the correct city.**

snow block	mud brick	cob

1.

adobe house

material _____

- made of mud, straw, sand, and water
- absorbs and releases heat slowly so that the house is cool during the day and warm at night

2.

igloo

material _____

- made of snow
- built to form a dome structure to trap heat inside

3.

cob house

material _____

- made of sand, clay, and water
- can absorb lots of water without softening

Nunavut, Canada
- very cold
- lots of snow

4.

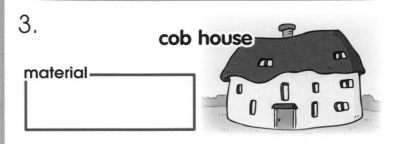

Devon, Britain
- mild temperature
- very wet

5.

Arizona, U.S.A.
- very hot
- can be very dry

6.

20

Sports and Recreation

People around the world enjoy sports and recreation. Some places are perfect for skiing and skating, while others are well known for surfing and fishing.

A. **Name the sports. Then draw lines to match the sports with the best places for them.**

soccer   surfing   skiing

- **Canada**

  long and cold winters;
  many snowy mountains

- **Britain**

  sunny and wet summers;
  lush grassland

- **Hawaii**

  hot and sunny;
  lots of beaches

B. Canada's natural environment favours a wide range of recreational activities. Match the activities with the correct places. Write the letters.

Recreational Activities

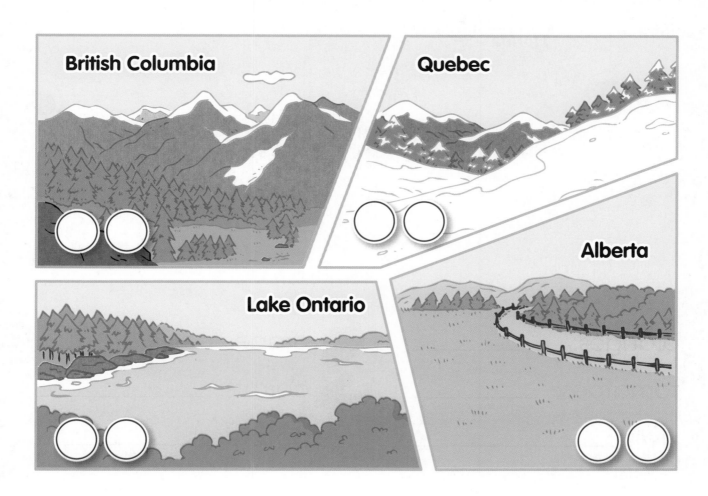

21

Foods from around the World

The foods we buy at grocery stores come from all over the world. Some places have climates that allow food crops to grow all year round.

A. **Look at the map. Find and write where the foods come from. Then check where the foods in your home come from and draw them on the map.**

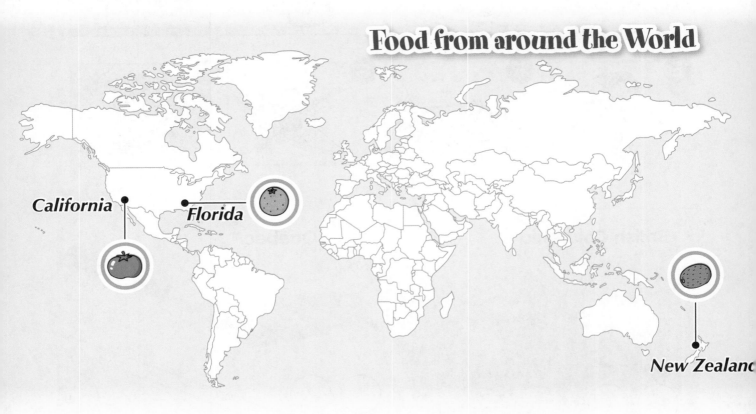

Food from around the World

California

Florida

New Zealand

Where They Come From

oranges: _____

tomatoes: _____

kiwis: _____

 grapes: _____

 carrots: _____

 potatoes: _____

B. Read the map of the food producers from around the world. Then answer the questions and circle the correct words.

Food Producers from around the World

Ecuador

Equator

Producer

1. Where are these food producers located on the map?

_____

2. Why do you think food crops are abundant in these locations?

_____

3.

Hello! My name is Juan. I live in Ecuador. The climate here is very **cold / hot** *, so* **bananas / grapes** *can grow well. We need deep, well-drained* **air / soil** *for the plants to stay healthy.*

Where People Live

There are many ways of finding information about the places we live in.

A. Look at the bar graph of the top ten most populated cities in Canada. Then answer the questions.

The Top Ten Most Populated Cities in Canada in 2011

Cities			
Ottawa, Ontario			
Toronto, Ontario			
Mississauga, Ontario			
Vancouver, British Columbia			
Brampton, Ontario			
Montreal, Quebec			
Edmonton, Alberta			
Calgary, Alberta			
Winnipeg, Manitoba			
Hamilton, Ontario			
0	1 million	2 million	3 million

Population

The top three most populated cities:

1: _____

2: _____

3: _____

In which province are most of these cities located?

_____

B. **Look at the cities in (A) again. Find and circle them on the map. Then answer the questions.**

1. What do you notice about the locations of the larger cities in Canada?

   _____

2. Why do you think most Canadians live in the southern part?

   _____

   _____

Adapting to a Place

People everywhere adapt or adjust to the location, climate, and special features of the land they live on.

A. Look at the pictures. Then write the letters in the correct boxes to show what the people say about the things they do to adapt to their environment.

A "We grow coconut palm trees because they grow well in hot and wet climates. It takes about a year for the trees to fruit."

B "We can cut through the ice to get our food."

C "We finish our work in the early morning when it's cooler."

Florida, U.S.A.
(humid and rainy; ground never freezes)

Managua, Nicaragua
(very hot during the day)

The Arctic
(frozen all year round)

B. People dress according to the weather. Choose the correct outfits and accessories for people in different parts of the world. Write the letters.

A tank-top

B cotton shirt

C umbrella

D sunscreen

E sunglasses

F woollen scarf

G mittens

H toque

I shorts

J rubber boots

K winter boots

L sandals

M lightweight pants

N goose down parka

O insulated pants

Managua, Nicaragua

Florida, U.S.A.

The Arctic

24

Preserving Our Resources

The world has many resources. Some places have rich soil to grow food, while others have minerals, oil, or fresh water. We have to work together to preserve our resources for future generations.

A. Look at the map. Answer the questions.

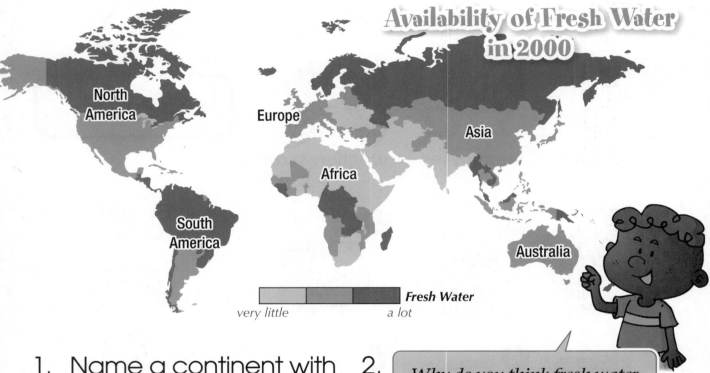

Availability of Fresh Water in 2000

North America

Europe

Asia

Africa

South America

Australia

very little   a lot   *Fresh Water*

1. Name a continent with

   a. a lot of fresh water

   _____

   b. some fresh water

   _____

   c. very little fresh water

   _____

2. *Why do you think fresh water is important to us?*

   _____

3. Write one thing you can do to help preserve our water.

   _____

   _____

B. **Match the people's actions with the results. Then answer the question.**

Results
- save electricity
- destroy forests
- grow own food

A We plant a garden in our yard, so we can have fresh vegetables all summer.

Result

B We turn off the lights when we leave a room.

Result

C We need a wider road here, so this forest has to be cleared.

Result

Which action above does not save our resources? Explain your choice.

_____

_____

SCIENCE

Animals

- Animals are classified into five major groups – reptiles, fish, amphibians, birds, and mammals.
- Mammals are animals that give birth to live young and feed them milk. Almost all mammals have fur or hair.

A. Colour the mammals in each group that have the described characteristics.

Characteristics of Mammals

- have fur or hair

- give birth to live babies

- feed its babies milk

B. The animals from different groups are describing their characteristics. Fill in the blanks to complete what they say. Then give two examples for each group.

birds   reptiles
amphibians   fish

alligator   goldfish   parrot   toad
salamander   turtle   shark   robin

1.

Snake

R_____ have scales or plates of armour. Their young hatch from eggs.

Examples _____ , _____

2.

Duck

B_____ lay eggs and have wings and feathers. Most can fly.

Examples _____ , _____

3.

Frog

A_____ live in water when they are young and on land when they are grown up.

Examples _____ , _____

4.

Clown fish

F_____ live in water and have fins to swim.

Examples _____ , _____

Ways Animals Eat and Move

- Animals have teeth and sometimes other body parts specially developed for the food they eat.
- Animals move in different ways, depending on what body parts they have.

A. Match the sentences with the animals. Write the letters.

Ⓐ My strong front teeth help me chew wood.

Ⓑ I have sharp teeth for the kill and chewing teeth too.

Ⓒ I munch grass in the pasture.

Ⓓ My teeth tear the flesh of my prey.

B. Some animals use other body parts for eating or reaching for food. Draw the missing body part on each animal.

1.

2.

C. **Each riddle is about an animal. Solve the riddle with the help of the pictures. Write the name of the animal on the line.**

1. *Two feet, two shoes*
   A pair of socks
   How do I move?
   I walk!

   _____

2. *Short legs on land*
   Make me waddle
   Webbed feet in water
   Help me paddle

   _____

3. *The place I move*
   Is in the sky
   My feathered wings
   Help me fly

   _____

4. *The shape of an S*
   From side to side
   I get there with
   A winding glide

   _____

5. *My body waves*
   My fins fan
   It's an underwater
   Travel plan

   _____

Animal Homes

- An animal has a home for protection from the sun, the cold, and its predators.
- Animal homes are different, depending on what the animals need.

Welcome.

A. **What does the home protect the animal from in each picture? Write "sun", "cold", or "predator" on the line.**

1.

My home is high above the ground.

_____

2.

_____

3.

_____

4.

_____

B. **Unscramble the letters to find the name of each animal's home.**

1. 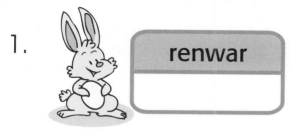 renwar

2.  ned

3.  orost

4. 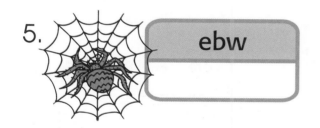 ehvi

5.  ebw

6.  gedol

C. **Match the birds with the correct nests.**

Winter Survival

- In fall, animals get ready for winter.
- Animals have different ways of adapting to cold weather to survive harsh winters.

It's not cold anymore by the fireplace.

A. Fill in the blanks with the given words. Then colour the correct pictures to match the sentences.

nuts   fur
feathers   slow

1. Fish _____ down in the water when the water temperature drops.

2. Ptarmigans grow extra _____ around their feet in winter.

3. Wolves' _____ grows thicker; it is their warm winter coat.

4. Squirrels gather and store _____ for winter meals.

B. Choose the correct answers to complete the sentences. Check ✔ the letters.

1. Hibernation is a way for some animals to

   (A) survive summer months.   (B) survive winter months.

2. During hibernation, an animal uses

   (A) less energy.   (B) more energy.

3. The heartbeat of a hibernating animal is

   (A) slower than normal.   (B) faster than normal.

C. Colour the hibernating animals.

5

Migration

- Animals migrate by air, land, or water to other places for many reasons, such as finding more food and better weather.
- Animals face many dangers when they migrate.

A. Match the route of migration with each animal. Colour the route and draw the picture in the circle.

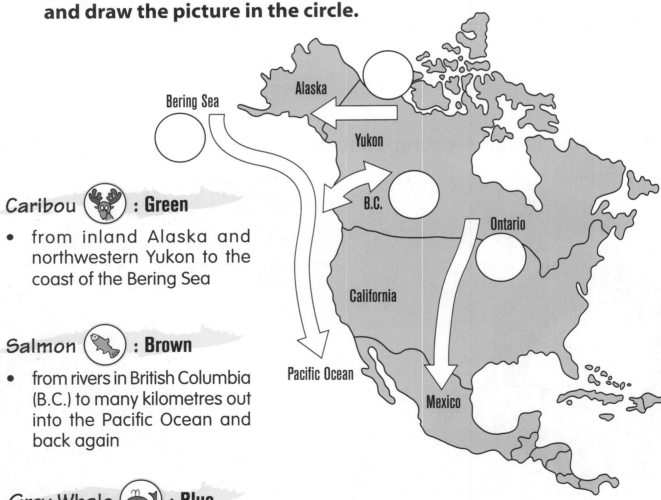

Bering Sea

Alaska

Yukon

B.C.

Ontario

California

Pacific Ocean

Mexico

Caribou : **Green**

- from inland Alaska and northwestern Yukon to the coast of the Bering Sea

Salmon : **Brown**

- from rivers in British Columbia (B.C.) to many kilometres out into the Pacific Ocean and back again

Grey Whale : **Blue**

- from the Bering Sea to southern California, staying close to the shoreline

Monarch Butterfly : **Orange**

- from Ontario overland to Mexico

B. Help the duck on her migration. Fill in the missing letters to find out the dangers.

1. po__ __ut__ __n

2. hu__t__rs

3. __to__ms

4. p__ed__t__ __s

C. Draw lines to tell how the animals migrate.

Ways to Migrate

by air	•
by water	•
by land	•

- monarch butterfly
- trumpeter swan
- garter snake
- grey whale
- giant sea turtle
- rufous hummingbird

6

Animal Babies

- Many baby animals have special names, but sometimes different animal babies share the same name.
- Animals care for their babies in different ways.

Isn't our baby cute?

A. Look at the picture clues. Complete the crossword puzzle with the names of the animal babies.

kangaroo

pig

dog

duck

sheep

swan

fish

deer

cygnet   duckling
fawn   fry
joey   lamb
piglet   puppy

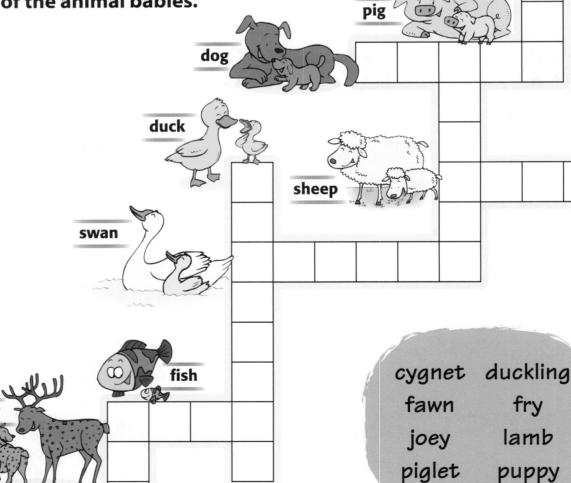

B. Write the letter for each group of animal babies in the correct circle.

A – foal   B – cub   C – calf

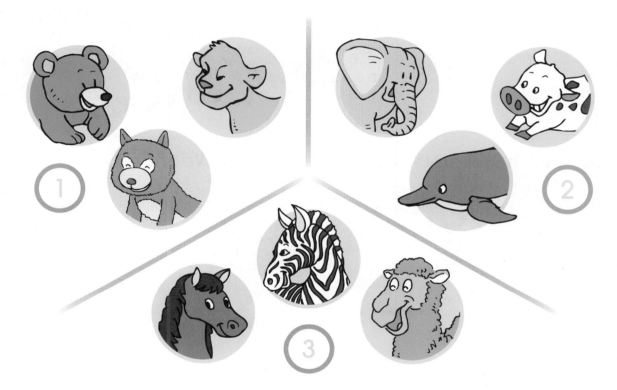

C. Match the correct descriptions with the animals. Write the letters.

A Some animals keep their baby in a pouch on the mother's body.

B Some animal babies are fed by both their mother and father.

C The young of some animals are on their own from birth.

D Some young animals travel on their parents' back.

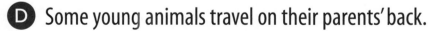

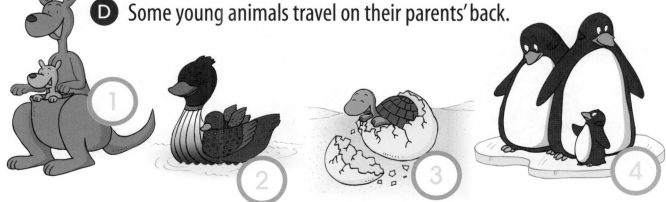

7

Animal Growth

- Animals get bigger as they grow, and sometimes they look different too.
- Animals can do different things as they grow.

We will fit into them one day.

A. Put the pictures in the correct order. Write 1 to 3.

1.

2.

3.

B. **The beluga whale changes its body colour when it grows. Fill in the missing letters to complete the colour words.**

- A newborn beluga whale is re___ ___ish br___ ___n.

- A young beluga whale is bl___ ___sh g___ ___y.

- An adult beluga whale is wh___t___ .

C. **See how the animals change with growth. Solve the riddles. Write the answers on the lines.**

a bird   **a mouse**   **a harp seal**

1. My pink, hairless body gets fur as it grows.
    My eyes will open, but right now they are closed.

    What am I?   _____

2. I am not like my mom; I have fluffy white fur.
    When it's smooth and grey, I'll be just like her.

    What am I?   _____

3. I'm featherless! Bring food to me!
    When I'm fully feathered, I'll leave this tree.

    What am I?   _____

8

Life Cycles

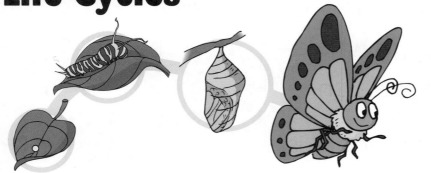

- *Some animals go through metamorphosis, or a complete change, during their life cycles.*

A. Name each stage of the life cycle for each animal.

Frog

tadpole   adult   egg

 ➡️  ➡️

_____   _____   _____

Dragonfly

adult   larva   egg

 ➡️ ➡️

_____   _____   _____

Butterfly

egg   chrysalis   caterpillar   adult

 ➡️  ➡️ ➡️

_____   _____   _____   _____

B. Read what Susan says. Help her match the correct caterpillar with the adult.

Caterpillars don't look like their parents, but sometimes they are similar in pattern or colour.

C. Circle the given words related to life cycles in the word search.

larva   metamorphosis   pupa   egg   adult   life cycle   caterpillar

z	x	c	c	v	b	n	m	l	k	j	h	g
m	e	t	a	m	o	r	p	h	o	s	i	s
q			t	e	r	b	u	i	o			x
a			e	f	h	j	p	l	m			v
b	l	a	r	v	a	r	a	y	t	b	n	e
f	g	h	p	u	t	w	e	c	v	b	o	g
a	s	l	i	f	e	c	y	c	l	e		g
r			l	t	u	f	b	w				u
t			l	o	k	d	s	g	h	j	t	y
i	r	e	a	w	q	a	a	d	u	l	t	e
u	i	p	r	l	k	j	g	f	d	s	a	q

9

Camouflage and Adaptation

- Some animals are naturally camouflaged. Their colours or patterns help them blend into their surroundings.
- Neither predator nor prey can easily see a camouflaged animal.

We're camouflaged.

A. Colour the animals that are camouflaged to help them blend into the habitats.

1.

tiger

hare

snake

2.

eagle

camel

hairy desert
scorpion

3.

polar bear

arctic fox

penguin

B. Find and colour the camouflaged animal in each picture.

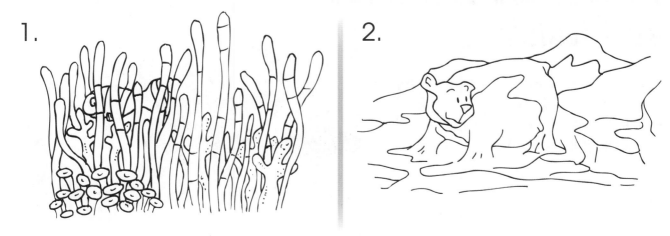

1.

2.

C. Write "predator" or "prey" to describe the camouflaged animals.

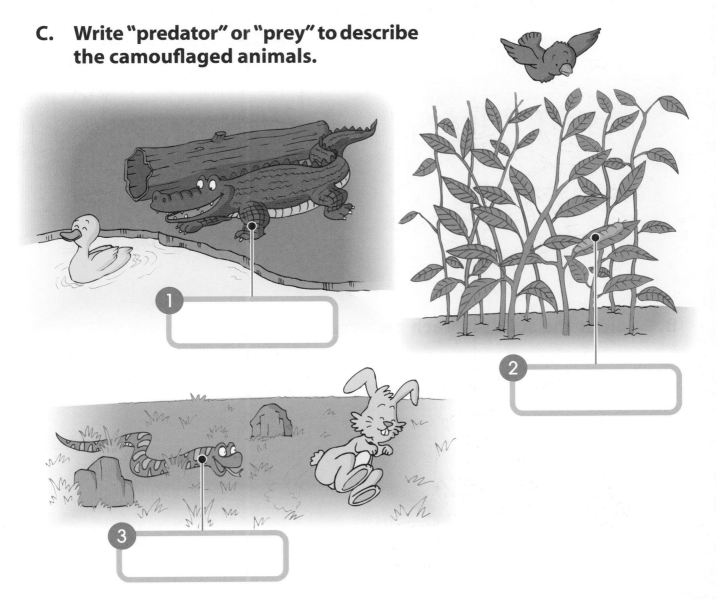

1

2

3

Properties of Liquids and Solids

- A solid has a shape that does not change easily.
- A liquid flows and takes the shape of its container.

A. Colour the liquids in each picture.

B. Colour the solids in each picture.

C. Help Mrs. Shaw draw lines to tell whether the things that she is going to buy are solids or liquids.

SUGAR

Milk

Detergent

Cookies

Tissues

Vegetable oil

• **Solids**

• **Liquids**

D. What is it? Write "solid" or "liquid" for each verse.

1

Pour it
Sip it
Swish it
Drip it

It is a _____ .

2

Knock it
Hold it
Turn it
Fold it

It is a _____ .

11

More about Liquids and Solids

- Some solids can dissolve in liquids, that is, they seem to disappear.
- Some solids can absorb, or soak up, liquids.

Look! It disappears.

A. Check ✔ the pictures that show a solid dissolving in a liquid.

B. Colour the solids that cannot dissolve in water.

C. **Mr. Soup has an accident. Help him clean up the spill. Colour the solids that will absorb liquids.**

D. **Circle the correct word in each sentence.**

1

A dishtowel absorbs / dissolves the water on wet dishes.

2

Salt absorbs / dissolves in a pot of tomato soup.

12

Three States of Water

- Water can be a liquid, a solid, or a gas.
- Heat and cold can change the state of water.

Mr. Water, which state are you in now?

A. Which state is the water in for each picture? Write "liquid", "solid", or "gas".

1 _____

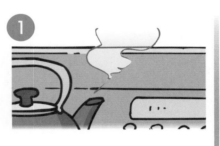

2 _____

3

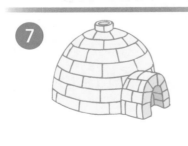

4 _____

5 _____

6 _____

7 _____

8 _____

B. **What will happen next? Fill in the blanks with "evaporate", "melt", or "freeze".**

1.

   The snowman will _____ .

2.

   The juice will _____ .

3.

   The soup will _____ .

C. **Read the clues. Complete the crossword puzzle.**

When ice melts, it turns to this.

Snow and ice are in this state.

Water turns to this when it is heated. →

This is formed when water freezes. →

The water we drink is in this state. →

water gas ice
liquid solid

13

Buoyancy

- When something can float on water, we say it is buoyant.
- We consider the buoyancy of a material when we make some things.

I like these new floating toys, Dad.

A. Colour the buoyant objects in the picture.

B. For each factory, choose the best material for the job. Write on the line.

- wood
- cork
- metal
- ice

1.

Rafts

_____

2.

Anchors

_____

C. **Colour the things that float to help Sam get across the river.**

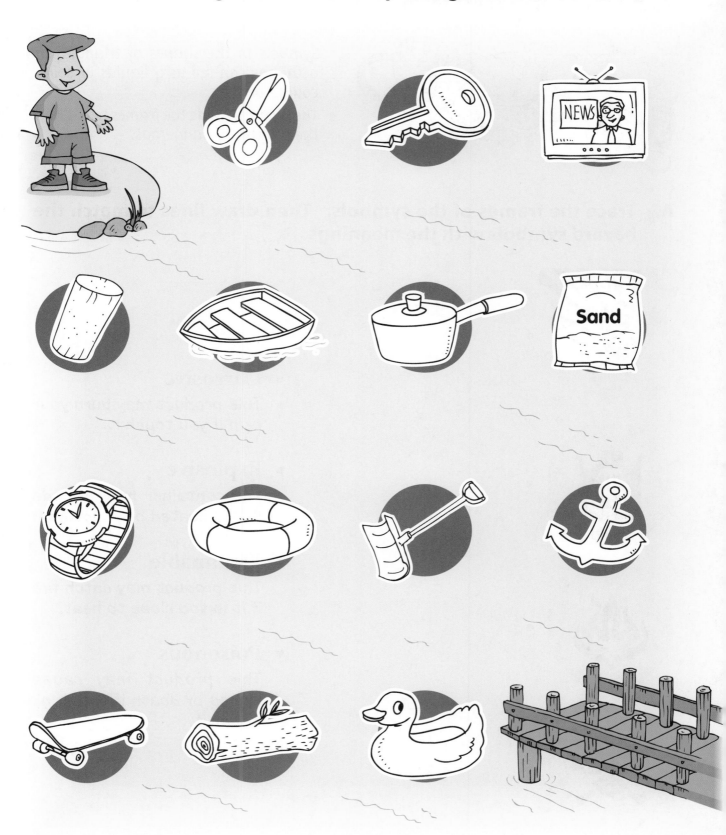

14

Hazard Symbols

- Symbols in the shapes of triangles or octagons can tell us if liquids or solids could harm us.
- The pictures inside the frames tell us how the things are dangerous.

A. Trace the frames of the symbols. Then draw lines to match the hazard symbols with the meanings.

- **Corrosive**
  This product may burn your skin if you touch it.

- **Explosive**
  The container may explode if it is heated or punctured.

- **Flammable**
  This product may catch fire if it is too close to heat.

- **Poisonous**
  This product may cause illness or death if you drink or eat it.

B. Match each label with the correct hazard symbol. Write the letter.

 A   B    C   D

Do not puncture container! Do not place near heat!

It may explode if it is heated or punctured.

1

Do not use or store near heat or flame!

It will catch fire easily if it is near heat.

2

Do not drink or eat!

It may cause illness or death if swallowed.

3

Do not touch with bare hands!

It may burn skin or eyes upon contact.

4

C. Colour the correct symbols. Then use the words that describe the symbols to complete the crossword puzzle.

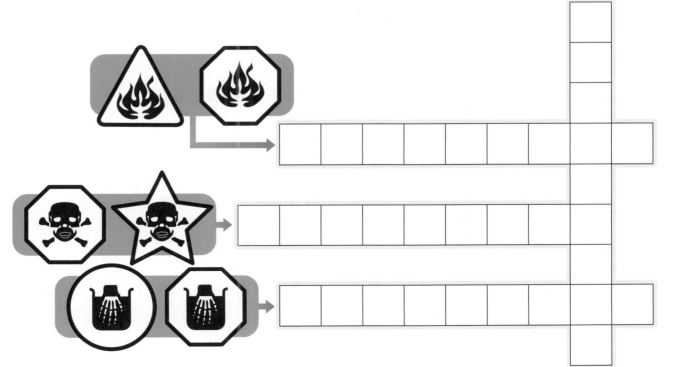

15

Air around Us

- Air is all around us. We cannot see it, but we know it is there when it takes up space or moves other things.
- We give moving air different names and dress ourselves in different ways, depending on the temperatures of the air.

A. Colour the correct objects to show the evidence of air.

1. **Air moves things:** objects being blown by the wind

2. **Air takes up space:** objects that have air inside them

B. Circle the different names for moving air in the word search.

e	S	t	■	A	z	u	h	i	S	X
b	r	e	e	z	e	h	a	f	a	g
■	k	l	P	q	p	w	r	e	n	c
m	g	a	l	e	h	r	m	Y	t	h
o	n	d	z	a	y	■	a	o	a	i
n	f	g	j	k	r	l	t	E	■	n
s	i	r	o	c	c	o	t	a	A	o
o	w	e	w	i	n	d	a	y	n	o
o	S	w	■	A	j	k	n	D	a	k
n	t	y	W	p	s	i	m	o	o	m
a	s	w	i	l	l	i	w	a	w	v

breeze
chinook
gale
harmattan
wind
monsoon
simoom
Santa Ana
sirocco
williwaw
zephyr

C. Complete the chart to tell what you do in cold and warm air temperatures.

	Cold Air	Warm Air
How I dress:		
Games I play:		
Sports I play:		
What I eat:		

Water around Us

Water is fun!

- Water can be found in different places and forms.
- Water goes through a cycle of evaporation and precipitation.

A. Where do we find water in our environment? Write the words on the lines.

river   lake
ocean   pond
ice   waterfall
underground

1 _____

2 _____

3 _____

4 _____

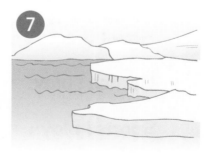

5 _____

6 _____

7 _____

B. Circle the forms of water around us in the word search.

snow fog frost
rain dew hail

f	e	r	d	e	w	t	h
o	f	r	o	s	t	y	a
g	b	n	m	n	g	u	i
c	v	x	z	o	k	i	l
r	a	i	n	w	p	o	l

C. Label the different stages of the water cycle in the natural environment. Then match them with the stages of the water cycle that you may find at home.

evaporation
condensation
precipitation

17

Clean Air and Water

- Living things need clean air and water for a healthy life, but many things we do cause air and water pollution.

A. **Cross out ✗ the pictures that show air or water pollution. Then colour the rest to show the girl and her friends the path to "clean air and water".**

B. Read each sign. Colour the right thing to do.

1.
Care about Air!

2.
Don't Waste Water!

3.
No More Litter!

4.
Save Our Ocean!

18

Energy Input and Output

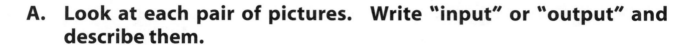

- The energy used to produce movement can be seen as an input, with the movement being the output.
- Many different types of energy can be used as input.

A. **Look at each pair of pictures. Write "input" or "output" and describe them.**

1.

input

Press the ___button___ .

_____

_____

2.

_____

_____

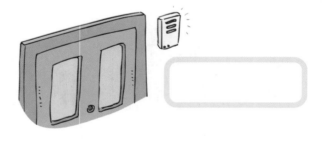

_____

_____

3.

_____

_____

_____

_____

B. **Label the sources of energy. Then match each source with the thing that depends on it to do work.**

food   electricity   fuel   wind

1.

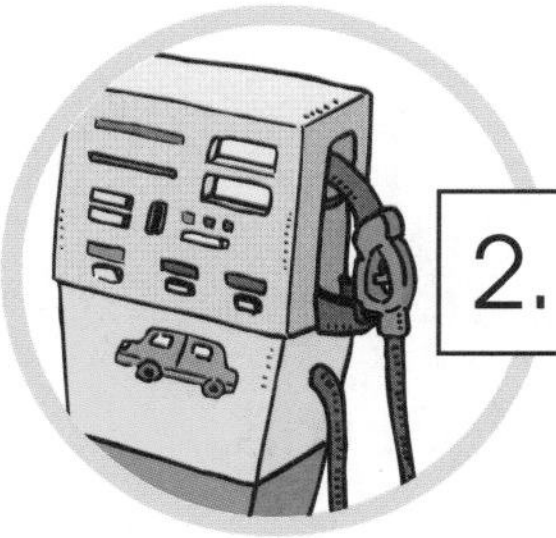

2.

3.

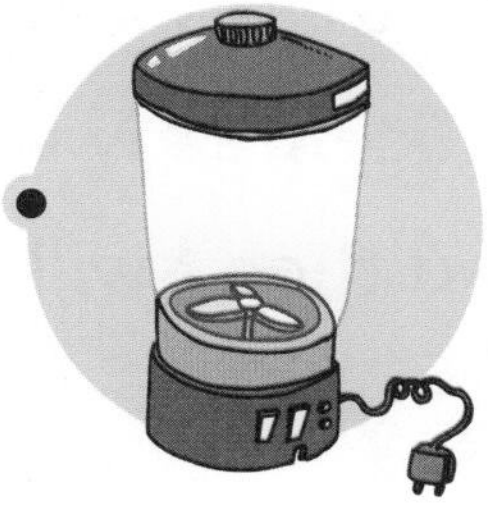

4.

C. **Find seven energy words on the previous page and this page. Write them on the lines.**

_____ _____ _____ _____

_____ _____ _____

19

Energy from Moving Water and Wind

- When air and water move, they become sources of energy.
- We have found many ways to use these sources of energy to do work for us.

A. Write the missing letters to complete the poems. Then match the poems with the correct pictures. Write the letters.

1. The surf is up,

   I'll catch a ___ave.

   This water moves fast,

   I have to be brave.

2. The sky is blue,

   The clouds are white.

   With the wind like this,

   I could fly my ___ite.

3. More than a breeze,

   Less than a gale.

   A nice steady wind,

   And then I will ___ail.

4. Down and up,

   Goes the sturdy craft.

   It's my third time now,

   On a white-water ___aft.

B. **Some of the pictures below show situations where moving water and wind are used as sources of energy. Match the pictures with the correct descriptions. Write the letters.**

A Moving water stops giving energy.

B Moving water gives energy.

C Wind stops giving energy.

D Wind gives energy.

1.

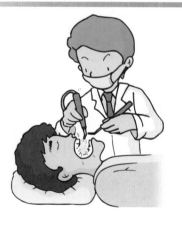

2.

3.

4.

C. **Use the given letters to complete the word to see what Mr. Earth wants to tell us.**

Energy from moving water and wind is __e__ew__ble, meaning that they are clean sources of energy and do no damage to me.

20

Windmills and Water Wheels

- Windmills and turbines are used to turn wind and moving water into sources of energy for us to use.
- The hydroelectric station is a place where the energy from moving water is changed into electrical energy.

A. Fill in the blanks with the given words to complete the passage.

boats   wind   saws   water
corn   windmills   electricity

1. _____ has been used by people as a source of energy for a long time. The Egyptians used it to sail their 2. _____ up and down the Nile River. The earliest 3. _____ were built in Persia around 600 CE. They were used to grind 4. _____ and pump 5. _____ up from the underground. Later on, people in Europe used windmills to power 6. _____ in sawmills and to grind grain. Windmills are still used today to produce 7. _____ .

B. Look at the "wheels" that use wind or moving water to produce energy. Write "wind" or "moving water" on the lines. Then answer the question.

1.

_____

2.

_____

3.

_____

4.

_____

5.

For the wheels that produce energy, describe what will happen if the water stops moving or the wind dies down.

_____

21

Positions

- *Some words help us describe where something is located.*
- *Other words tell us which way something moves.*

Amy **Janet** **Linda**

Janet is between Amy and me.

A. Colour the toys.

The toy(s)

- **behind a top** – green
- **above the dinosaur** – blue
- **under the soldier** – yellow
- **beside the kite and on a box** – pink
- **between the ball and the mouse** – grey
- **in front of a robot** – orange
- **in a box** – purple
- **over a top** – red

B. **Find all the position words in (A). Write them on the lines.**

_____   _____   _____

_____   _____   _____

_____   _____   _____

C. **Read the directions and draw a path Rebecca must take to get her hat.**

- around the swings
- up the ladder
- through the tunnel
- down the slide
- over the rocking horse
- under the bench

Movements

- A *pattern of movement* is the way something repeatedly moves.

A. Identify the patterns of movement in the sports. Write the correct words on the lines.

Spinning is fun!

bouncing   sliding   spinning   zigzagging
rolling   swinging   turning

1   _____

2   _____

3   _____

4   _____

6   _____

7   _____

5   _____

B. **Read what the children say. Match the children with their favourite rides. Write the letters.**

1. I was sliding down my ride.

2. I feel really dizzy from turning.

3. My ride was twisting! It was great.

4. I feel like I'm still swinging on my ride!

5. I bounced!

C. **Describe the patterns of movement involved in these kitchen objects.**

turn
slide
roll

1.

2.

3.

Simple Machines

- Simple machines make our work easier.

> I can move this rock easily by using a stick and a small rock.

A. **Write what kind of simple machine each tool is. Then choose the correct tool to do each job. Write the letter.**

| inclined plane | wedge | lever |
| wheel and axle | screw | pulley |

A _____

B _____

C _____

D _____

E _____

F _____

Keep the door **Open**

Flour

1

2

3

4

5

6

B. Cross out ✗ the things that are not examples of levers.

Examples of Levers

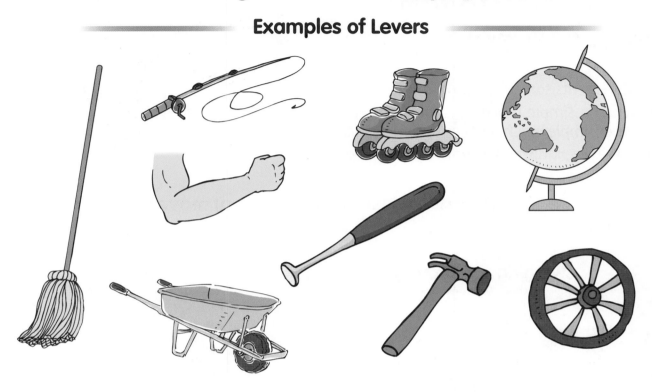

C. Use the name of the store as a clue to tell what is in each box.

wedges   levers
wheels and axles

The
Knives and Axe Blades
Place

1. _____

Wagonland

2. _____

Teeter-Totters
and More!

3. _____

Movements and Mechanisms

a turning head

a vibrating tail

- Movements sometimes form a pattern.
- When a simple machine is joined to at least one other simple machine, they become a mechanism.
- Some mechanisms help us move things more easily.

A. Use the given words to describe the types of movements involved in each picture.

| swinging | vibrating | turning | spinning | bouncing |

1.

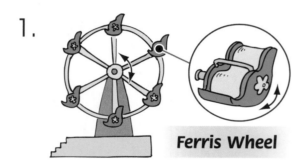

Ferris Wheel

- a big _____ wheel
- some _____ chairs

2.

Alarm Clock

- a _____ hammer
- _____ clock hands

3.

Push Toy

- some _____ balls
- a _____ base

4.

Sewing Machine

- a _____ needle
- a _____ thread coil

B. **Circle the three mechanisms in Matt's collection.**

C. **Identify the simple machine paired with the lever in each mechanism. Then tell what movement is made easier.**

screw   wedge   pulling   pushing   turning

1
• _____ + lever
Movement made easier: _____

2
• _____ + lever
Movement made easier: _____

3
• _____ + lever
Movement made easier: _____

ANSWERS

1 Numbers to 20

1. 13
2. 16
3. 9
4. 5
5. 17
6. 8
7. fourteen
8. eight
9. sixteen
10. nineteen
11. twenty
12. eleven
13. seven
14. twelve
15.

16. 15
17. 18
18. 11
19. 5, 6, 10, 11
20. 9, 14, 17, 20
21. 8, 13, 15, 19
22. 5, 12, 16, 18
23. 10 ; 11 ; 13 ; 14 ; 16 ; 17
24. 15 ; 13 ; 12 ; 10 ; 8 ; 7
25. 12 ; 13 ; 16 ; 17 ; 19 ; 20
26. 12
27. 7
28. 5
29. 16
30. 1
31. 11
32. 5
33. 8
34. 11
35. in all ; 12 ;
$$\begin{array}{r} 7 \\ + \ 5 \\ \hline 1\,2 \end{array}$$
36. have left ; 7 ;
$$\begin{array}{r} 1\,6 \\ - \ 9 \\ \hline 7 \end{array}$$
37. more ; than ; 13 ;
$$\begin{array}{r} 9 \\ + \ 4 \\ \hline 1\,3 \end{array}$$
38. have left ; 4 ;
$$\begin{array}{r} 1\,2 \\ - \ 8 \\ \hline 4 \end{array}$$

2 Numbers 21 to 100

1. 48
2. 36
3. 15
4. 19
5. 78
6. 56

7. 60, 57, 49, 42
8. 84, 80, 68, 48
9. 53, 50, 35, 33
10.
   a. 16
   b. 32
11.
   a. 7
   b. 35
12. 12
13. 7
14. 40
15. 100
16. 90
17. 35
18. 20 ; 35 ; 40
19. 30 ; 50 ; 90
20. 50 ; 52 ; 58
21. 4 ; 3 ; 43 ;

22. 5 ; 2 ; 52 ;

23. 7 ; 3
24. 28
25. 6 ; 5
26. 91
27. 32

3 Addition of 2-Digit Numbers

1. 47
2. 64
3. 39
4. 89
5. 97
6. 85
7. 85
8. 72
9. 38
10. 87
11. 38
12. 77
13. 49
14. 39
15. 72
16. 66
17. 56
18. 99
19.
$$\begin{array}{r} ① \\ 3\,5 \\ + \ 2\,8 \\ \hline 6\,3 \end{array}$$
20.
$$\begin{array}{r} ① \\ 4\,7 \\ + \ 2\,9 \\ \hline 7\,6 \end{array}$$
21.
$$\begin{array}{r} ① \\ 1\,8 \\ + \ 5\,4 \\ \hline 7\,2 \end{array}$$
22.
$$\begin{array}{r} ① \\ 4\,3 \\ + \ 3\,9 \\ \hline 8\,2 \end{array}$$

23.
```
  ①
  2 4
+ 2 9
  5 3
```
24.
```
  ①
  6 3
+ 1 7
  8 0
```

25. 56　　　　26. 84
27. 70　　　　28. 63
29.

```
  2 4        5 3        4 8
+ 1 9      + 3 7      + 4 8
  4 3        9 0        9 6
```

62 + 28 = __90__　　25 + 16 = __41__

9 + 49 = __58__　　33 + 8 = __41__

30. a.
```
      ↓
30   32   35      40
```
　　b. 30 ; 30

31. a.
```
               ↓
60       65   69 70
```
　　b. 70 ; 70

32. a.
```
        ↓
40    44 45     50
```
　　b. 40 ; 40

33. 92 ;
```
    4 0
  + 5 0
    9 0
```
34. 65 ;
```
    5 0
  + 2 0
    7 0
```

35. 93 ;
```
    8 0
  + 1 0
    9 0
```
36. 83 ;
```
    6 0
  + 2 0
    8 0
```

37. 52 ;
```
    1 4
  + 3 8
    5 2
```
38. 52 ;
```
    4 6
  +   6
    5 2
```

39. 74 ;
```
    3 7
  + 3 7
    7 4
```
40. 36 + 36 ; 72 ; 72

4　Subtraction of 2-Digit Numbers

1. 34　　　　2. 61
3. 53　　　　4. 53
5. 41　　　　6. 4
7. 12　　　　8. 12
9. 13
10.
```
    3 8   ; 23
  - 1 5
    2 3
```
11.
```
    7 5   ; 63
  - 1 2
    6 3
```
12. 28　　　　13. 39
14. 16　　　　15. 34
16. 32　　　　17. 8

18. 18　　　　19. 18
20. 17　　　　21. 25
22. 14　　　　23. 18
24. a.
```
    9 4   ; 55
  - 3 9
    5 5
```
b.
```
    4 6   ; 7
  - 3 9
      7
```

25. a.
```
  32              49
  30    40    50
```
　　b. 30 ; 50　　　c. 17 ;
```
    5 0
  - 3 0
    2 0
```

26. a.
```
  76          93
  70    80   90   100
```
　　b. 80 ; 90　　　c. 17 ;
```
    9 0
  - 8 0
    1 0
```

27. 28 ;
```
    5 0
  - 2 0
    3 0
```
28. 18 ;
```
    7 0
  - 5 0
    2 0
```

29. 24 ;
```
    6 0
  - 3 0
    3 0
```
30. 35 ;
```
    8 0
  - 5 0
    3 0
```

31. A: 61 ; B: 43 ; C: 76
32. C
33. B　　　　34. 18 ;
```
    6 1
  - 4 3
    1 8
```

35. 33 ;
```
    7 6
  - 4 3
    3 3
```
36. 34 ;
```
    5 0
  - 1 6
    3 4
```

5　More about Addition and Subtraction

1. 85 ;
```
    5 0
  + 4 0
    9 0
```
2. 38 ;
```
    6 0
  - 3 0
    3 0
```

3. 24 ;
```
    5 0
  - 3 0
    2 0
```
4. 95 ;
```
    1 0
  + 8 0
    9 0
```

5. 51 ;
```
    7 0
  - 2 0
    5 0
```
6. 85 ;
```
    8 0
  + 1 0
    9 0
```

7. ✔ ; 95　　　　8. ✘ ; 45 ;
```
    2 9
  + 5 5
    8 4
```

9. ✔ ;
```
    2 8
  + 3 9
    6 7
```
10. ✘ ; 38 ;
```
    1 4
  + 4 8
    6 2
```

11. ✘ ; 29 ;
```
    4 9
  + 2 7
    7 6
```
12. ✘ ; 25 ;
```
    1 6
  + 3 5
    5 1
```

13. 38 ;
$$\begin{array}{r} 75 \\ -\ 37 \\ \hline 38 \end{array}$$
;
$$\begin{array}{r} 37 \\ +\ 38 \\ \hline 75 \end{array}$$

14. 57 ;
$$\begin{array}{r} 61 \\ -\ \ 4 \\ \hline 57 \end{array}$$
;
$$\begin{array}{r} 4 \\ +\ 57 \\ \hline 61 \end{array}$$

15. 66 ;
$$\begin{array}{r} 82 \\ -\ 16 \\ \hline 66 \end{array}$$
;
$$\begin{array}{r} 16 \\ +\ 66 \\ \hline 82 \end{array}$$

16. 47 ;
$$\begin{array}{r} 96 \\ -\ 49 \\ \hline 47 \end{array}$$
;
$$\begin{array}{r} 49 \\ +\ 47 \\ \hline 96 \end{array}$$

17. 56 ; 17 ; 73
73 ; 17 ; 56
73 ; 56 ; 17

18. 28 ; 62 ; 90
62 ; 28 ; 90
90 ; 62 ; 28

19. 43 + 27 ; 70
27 + 43 ; 70
70 − 43 ; 27
70 − 27 ; 43

20. 14 + 32 ; 46
32 + 14 ; 46
46 − 14 ; 32
46 − 32 ; 14

21. 67 + 15 ; 82
15 + 67 ; 82
82 − 67 ; 15
82 − 15 ; 67

5. A: 14   B: 12
C: 17   D: 11
6. D   7. C
8. A: 15 ; 8
B: 5 ; 6
C: 3:00 ; 3 o'clock
D: 6:30 ; half past 6
9. a.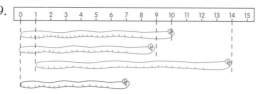
b. 1
10. a.
b. 30
11. A: 18 ; B: 0 ; C: 27 ;
From top to bottom: C ; B ; A
12.  ; drop ; lower

6 Time and Temperature

1.

Judy's Schedule	July the month right after June		2014 the year right after 2013			
SUN	MON	TUE	WED	THU	FRI	SAT
		1	2	3	☀	☀
☀	☀	☀	☀	☀	11	12
13	14	15	16	17	18	19
20	21	22	23	24	25	26
27	28	29	30	31		

2. July 4 ; July 10 ; 7 ; 1
3. July 15 ; July 28 ; 14 ; 2
4.

```
        D
  O     E
  C     C     M
  T     E     A
N O V E M B E R
  B     B     C
  E     E     H
  R     R
```

7 Length

1. (Individual answers)
2. C   3. D
4. a. 10 ; 12   b.
5. a. 2 ; 16   b.
6. A: longer ; 10 cm
B: shorter ; 9 cm
C: 13 cm
7. C
8. 3 cm
9.

10.
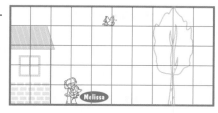

11. 4 ; 5
12. taller
13. 1 m
14. 5 m
15. 4 m
16. 2 m
17. 3 m

8 Perimeter and Area

1. A ; B ; D
2. A: 22   B: 18
   C: 12   D: 12
   E: 6   F: 8
3. A: 15   B: 21
   C: 36   D: 20
4. ✦
5. smaller
6 and 8.

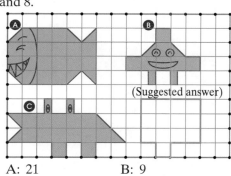

(Suggested answer)

A: 21   B: 9
C: 16
7. A

9 Money

1. 1 ; Loonie
2. 25 ; Quarter
3. 1 ; Penny
4. 10 ; Dime
5. 2 ; Toonie
6. 5 ; Nickel
7. A, C
8. A, B
9. 83¢
10. 60¢
11. (25¢) (10¢) (10¢) (1¢) (1¢) (1¢)
12. (25¢) (25¢) (10¢) (5¢) (1¢)

13. (25¢) (25¢) (25¢) (10¢) (1¢) (1¢)

14-15. (Suggested answers)
14. (10¢) (10¢) (10¢) (10¢) (10¢) (10¢) (10¢) (1¢)
15. (25¢) (10¢)

16.

17.

18.

19.

20. (25¢) (25¢) (25¢) (5¢) (5¢) (1¢) (1¢) (1¢) (1¢) ;
    89
21. (25¢ ✗) (25¢) (10¢) (10¢) (10¢) (5¢) (5¢) (1¢) (1¢) ;
    67

10 Addition and Subtraction with Money

1. 65
2.   25¢
   + 19¢
   ─────
      44¢
3.   49¢
   + 38¢
   ─────
      87¢
4.   27¢
   + 27¢
   ─────
      54¢
5.   19¢
   + 49¢
   ─────
      68¢
6.   25¢
   + 38¢
   ─────
      63¢

7.
```
   19¢
 + 19¢
   38¢
```

8.
```
   27¢
 + 49¢
   76¢
```

9.
```
   25¢
 + 49¢
   74¢
```

10. 6

11.
```
   75¢
 - 68¢
    7¢
```

12. 48

13.
```
   80¢
 - 16¢
   64¢
```

14. 24¢ ; 21¢ ; 49¢ ; 36¢
15. 67¢ ; 16¢ ; 32¢ ; 25¢
16. a. 80   b. 62¢ ;
```
   80¢
 - 18¢
   62¢
```

17. a. 70   b. 24¢ ;
```
   70¢
 - 46¢
   24¢
```

18. a. 24 ; 55   b. 79¢ ;
```
   24¢
 + 55¢
   79¢
```

19. 75 – 16 ; 59 ;

20. 36 + 59 ; 95 ;

21. 37 + 43 ; 80 ;

11 2-D Shapes (1)

1. 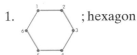 ; hexagon

2. ; triangle

3. ; square

4. ; rectangle

5. ; pentagon

6. 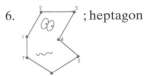 ; heptagon

7.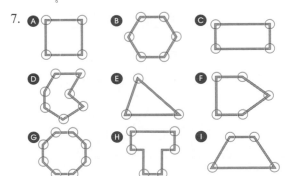

8. a. F   b. Yes
9. a. A, C, I   b. 4
10. (Suggested answer)

11. 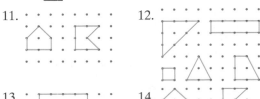 12.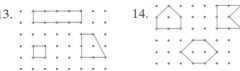

13.  14.

15-16. (Individual designs)
15. circle ; triangle
16. hexagon ; rectangle
17. 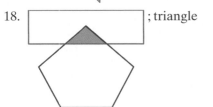 ; square

18. ; triangle

19. ; pentagon

12 2-D Shapes (2)

1. B, D
2. A, C
3. C, E
4. A: triangle   B: triangle
   C: triangle   D: square
   E: triangle   F: parallelogram
   G: triangle

5-6.

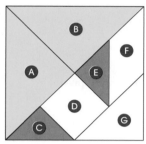

7. 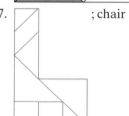 ; chair

8.  ; fish

9. Check ✔ the pictures A, C, E, and F.
   A: 3 ; tree
   C: 7 ; candle
   E: 3 ; boat
   F: 7 ; hexagon

10.

11.

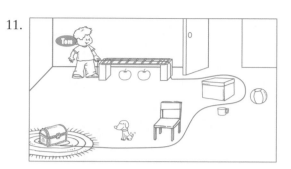

13 Symmetry

1.

2.
3.

4.
5.

6.
7.

8.
9.

10.

11. 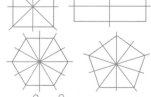 ; 4 ; 2 ; 5 ; 6

12.

13.

14.

15.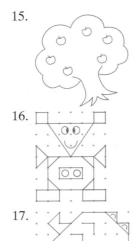

16.

17.

18-20. (Suggested answers)
18. This symmetrical design looks like a candy.
19. There are 5 triangles, 1 circle, and 1 rectangle in this symmetrical design.
20. There are 2 triangles, 6 small circles, 1 big circle, and 2 rectangles in this symmetrical design.

21.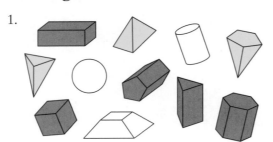

14 3-D Figures

1.

2. cube   3. prism
4. pyramid
5.  ; cone ; prism

6.  ; sphere ; cube

7. 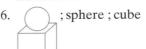 ; pyramid ; cylinder

8. ; pyramid ; prism

9. square
10. triangle
11. pentagon
12. triangle
13. rectangle
14. triangle
15. B ;
    A, C, D, E, F
16. C, D, E, F ;
    A, B
17. A, B, E, F ;
    C, D
18. 2   19. 4 ; 1
20. 12 ; 8   21. 10 ; 6
22. 9 ; 6   23. 12 ; 7
24. pyramid ; 8 ; 5

15 Multiplication (1)

1. ; 2 ; 2 ; 6 ; 12

2. ; 4 ; 5 ; 4 ; 20

3. ; 3 ; 5 ; 5 ; 15

4. 5 ; 5 ;
   5 ; 5 ; 30
5. 3 ; 3 ; 3 ; 3 ;
   8 ; 3 ; 8 ; 3 ; 24

6. 4 ; 4 ; 4 ; 4 ;
   7 ; 4 ; 7 ; 4 ; 28

7.

8.

9.
0 2 4 6 8 10 12 14 16 18 20

10.
0 5 10 15 20 25 30 35 40 45 50

11.
0 10 20 30 40 50 60 70 80 90 100

12. 2 ; 4 ; 6 ; 8 ; 10 ; 12 ; 14 ; 16 ; 18 ; 20
13. 5 ; 10 ; 15 ; 20 ; 25 ; 30 ; 35 ; 40 ; 45 ; 50
14. 10 ; 20 ; 30 ; 40 ; 50 ; 60 ; 70 ; 80 ; 90 ; 100
15. a. 6   b. 27
    c. 21   d. 15
    e. 12   f. 9
16. a. 24   b. 20
    c. 28   d. 36
    e. 12   f. 16
17. 20 ;

16 Multiplication (2)

1. 6 ; 12 ; 18 ; 24 ; 30 ; 36 ; 42 ; 48 ; 54 ; 60
2. 7 ; 14 ; 21 ; 28 ; 35 ; 42 ; 49 ; 56 ; 63 ; 70
3. a. 32   b. 16
   c. 64   d. 56
   e. 24   f. 48
   g. 72
4. 10 x 8 ; 80 ; 80
5. a. 45   b. 18
   c. 63   d. 54
   e. 81   f. 72
   g. 9
6. 4 x 9 ; 36 ; 36   7. 28
8. 18   9. 80
10. 36   11. 48
12. 27   13. 14
14. 32   15. 63
16. 42   17. 24

18. 54
19. A: 45   B: 48
    C: 49   D: 18
    E: 18
20. C   21. B
22. 54 ; 9   23. 56 ; 8
        x 6   x 7
        54   56
24. 48 ; 6   25. 28 ; 7
        x 8   x 4
        48   28
26. 36 ; 6
        x 6
        36

17 More about Multiplication

1. 1 ; 1 ; 1 ; 6 ; 6
2. 0 ; 0 ; 5 ; 0
3. 0 ; 0 ; 7 ; 0
4. 1 ; 1 ; 4 ; 4
5. 12   6. 0   7. 9
8. 12   9. 0   10. 21
11. 2   12. 32   13. 10
14. 18   15. 49   16. 20
17. 0   18. 3   19. 6
20. 14   21. 0
22. 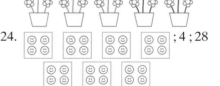 ; 2 ; 12
23.  ; 5 ; 15
24. ; 4 ; 28
25. 6 ; 24
26. 7 ; 21
27. 5 ; 40
28. 9 ; 36
29. ; 2
30. ; 3

18 Division

1.  ; 12 ; 3

2.  ; 20 ; 4

3. 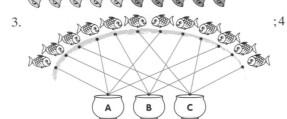 ; 4

4. 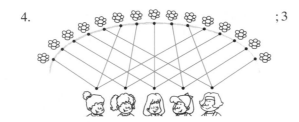 ; 3

5. a. 12   b. 4
6. a. 20   b. 4
7. a.

   b. 6   c. 3
8.  ; 7 ; 21 ; 21 ; 3

9. ; 6 ; 24 ; 24 ; 4

10. 5

19 Fractions (1)

1.
2.
3.
4.

5.
6.
7.
8.
9.
10. A, D

11. B, C   12. A, D
13. three   14. one fourth
15. four fifths   16. one half
17. two thirds   18. five eighths
19. a-b.   c. Two thirds

20. a-b.

   c. Three fourths
21. 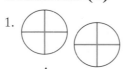 ; Two thirds

22. ; Five sixths

23. one ; one fourth ; 4 ;

24. one third ; one sixth ; 6 ;

25.  ; Two fourths is bigger.

20 Fractions (2)

1. a. Four
   b. fourths

2. a. Three
   b. thirds
   c. two

3.
   a. Eight
   b. two
   c. Four

4.

5.

6.

7. Combine eight fifths to form one whole and three fifths.
8. Combine sixteen sixths to form two wholes and four sixths.
9. a.
   b. greater   c. smaller
10. a.
   b. smaller   c. smaller
11. one half
12. four sixths
13. two thirds
14. two sixths
15. a.
   b. Three fifths ; one third
16. a.
   b. One half ; two tenths ; three fourths
17. one tenth

21 Capacity

1. 2. 3. 4. 5. 6.

7. C, A, B
8. C, B, A
9. D, C, A, B
10-11. (Suggested answers)
  10.
  11.
12. C   13. B
14. C   15. 4
16.    17.
18. a spoon   19. a pail
20. a cup
21-24. (Suggested answers)
  21. a cup
  22. a spoon
  23. a water bottle
  24. a cup

22 Mass

1. 2. 3. 4.

5. the dog   6. the dog
7. the bird   8. the dog
9. 4   10. 4 ; 2
11. the tree: 5   the pig: 7
    the nutcracker: 2   the gift: 1
    the rocket: 2
12.

13. 1   14. 2
15.   16.

17.

18.

23 Patterns (1)

1. ✔ ; 🍎
2. ✗
3. ✔ ; 😀
4. ✔ ; 20
5. ✔ ; ▭
6. ○○●●○○○ ; growing
7. 45 50 55 60 65 70 75 80 85 ; growing
8. AAAAAAA AAAAAA AAAAA AAAA AAA AA ; shrinking
9.  ;

growing

10-12. (Suggested answers)

10. 🎉🎉🎩🎉🎉🎩
11. 🌷❀🌷🌷❀🌷
12. 🙂🙁😖🙂😖🙁
13. 13 + 5 = 18 ; growing
14. 70 − 5 = 65 ; shrinking

15-16. (Suggested answers)

15. 🙁🙁🙁 🙁🙁🙁 🙁🙁🙁 🙁🙁🙁 ; 8 ; 6 ; 6
16. 🙂🙂🙂🙂🙂🙂🙂 🙂🙂🙂🙂🙂🙂 ; 5 ; 6 ; 7

17. 6
18. 2
19. 8
20. 4
21. 10
22. 6
23. 2

24 Patterns (2)

1. 61, 62, 63, 64, 65, 66, 67, 68, 69, 70 ; row
2. 8, 18, 28, 38, 48, 58, 68, 78, 88, 98 ; column
3. shrinking

4-6.

1	2	③	4	5	6	7	8	9	10
11	12	⑬	14	15	16	17	18	19	20
21	22	㉓	24	25	26	27	28	29	30
31	32	㉝	34	35	36	37	38	39	40
41	42	㊸	44	45	46	47	48	49	50
51	52	㊾	54	55	56	57	58	59	60
61	62	㊿	64	65	66	67	68	69	70
71	72	73	74	75	76	77	78	79	80
81	82	83	84	85	86	87	88	89	90
91	92	93	94	95	96	97	98	99	100

4. row
5. column
6. 83 ; 78 ; 73 ; 68 ; Yes ; 63, 58
7. 🪑 ; shape
8. 👣 ; size
9. 🐱 ; pattern
10. 📶 ; position
11. colour ; orientation
12. pattern ; size
13. position ; shape
14. orientation ; pattern
15. big, big, small ; zigzag, wave

25 Organizing Data

1. Big Bag of Cheese Popcorn: A, F, H
   Small Bag of Cheese Popcorn: C, I, J
   Big Bag of Caramel Popcorn: D, E
   Small Bag of Caramel Popcorn: B, G

2-5. (Individual colouring and sorting)

6. A: With Hood: ‖‖‖‖ ‖‖‖ ;
   Without Hood: ‖‖‖ ‖‖
   B: Black: ‖‖‖ ;
   Blue: ‖‖‖ ‖ ;
   Red: ‖‖‖
   C: Black Jumper with Hood: ‖ ;
   Blue Jumper with Hood: ‖‖‖ ;
   Red Jumper with Hood: ‖ ;
   Black Jumper without Hood: ‖‖ ;
   Blue Jumper without Hood: ‖ ;
   Red Jumper without Hood: ‖‖

7. A
8. C

9-11. (Individual colouring and answers)

Shoes			A	B	C	D	E	F	G	H	I	J	K	L
Colour	Blue													
	Brown													
Type	Women's	With Shoelaces		✔					✔					
		Without Shoelaces	✔			✔							✔	✔
	Men's	With Shoelaces						✔	✔		✔	✔		
		Without Shoelaces			✔	✔								

26 Pictographs

1. swimming
2. skating
3. 2
4. 23
5. 3
6. 6
7. 6
8. marbles with a cat's eye
9. 23
10. Circle: ⊞⊞ ; Rectangle: ⊞⊞ ;
    Square: ||||; Triangle: ⊞⊞ |||
11.
Number of Shapes Made

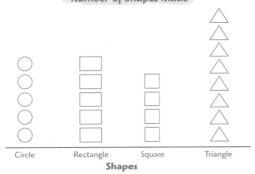

12. 22
13. triangle
14.
Ice Cream Cones the Children Ate Last Month

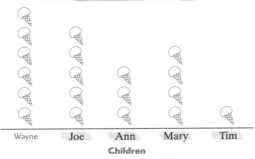

15. Wayne, because he ate the most ice cream cones.

27 Bar Graphs

1. 4
2. 2
3. French fries
4. 19
5. Number of Boxes of Doughnuts Sold
6. walnut crunch
7. strawberry
8. 16
9. 4

10. Hamburger: ⊞⊞ ||| ; Salad: |||| ;
    Chicken burger: |||| ; French fries: ⊞⊞ || ;
    Fish burger: |||| Onion rings: ⊞⊞
11. A
12.
The Children's Lunch Tomorrow

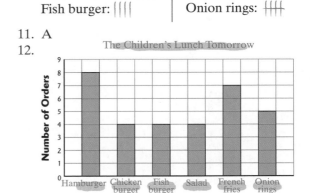

13. 8
14. 7
15. 4
16. 16

28 Probability

1. a. impossible   b. likely
2. a. impossible   b. certain
3. a. unlikely   b. impossible
4. a. equally   b. more
5. a. more   b. less
6. a. more   b. less
7-9. (Suggested colouring and answers)
7.

   b. red ; blue
8.

   b. yellow ; red
9.

   b. yellow / green
10. Colour the spinners as specified.
11. A: green or red ;   B: green, red, or blue ;
    C: red, blue, or yellow
12. No   13. Yes
14. Yes   15. Yes
16.

1 Say It with Flowers

A. 1.
Thank you.

2.
I love you.

3.
I think of you every day.

B.

```
                              ┌─F─┐
      ❶                       │ L │
    ┌─D─┐              ❷      │ O │
    │ A │            ┌─V─┐    │ W │
    │ I │            │ I │    │ E │
  Ⓐ │ S U N F L O W E R │    │ R │
  Ⓑ L I L Y │          │ L │    │ S │
    └───┘    Ⓒ C R O S E T │
                        │ T │
```

C. 1. 2.

3. 4.

5. 6.

D.

v	i	n	a	r	h	m	o	c	g	k
x	c	p	z	b	r	u	s	h	t	p
t	r	e	e	w	t	y	f	w	l	r
f	a	u	j				r	d	p	a
z	y	e	d				o	s	a	w
s	o	m	r	q	d	r	g	h	x	n
l	n	g	u	g	r	a	p	e	s	u
y	c	t	m	v	b	s	e	o	k	j

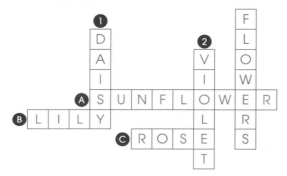

E. 1. sc
   2. st
   3. sw
   4. sp
   5. sm
   6. sk
   7. sn

2 Tongue Twisters

A.

					d	f	i	s	h	u	b	k	b
			q	s	t	g	p	h	i	g	n	p	u
	p	i	c	k	e	d	s	z	o	p	s	b	i g
m	j	h	a	d	l	p	e	p	p	e	r	s	c	v
c	r	o	s	m	l	w	a	x	c	c	h	w	k	a
l	b	i	t	y	s	l	s	f	n	k	q	e	l	f
e	o	w	o	o	d	c	h	u	c	k	j	k	e	s
	j	p	r	n	v	e	s	i	h	t	i	d	a
k	b	p	t	l	b	l	a	c	k	b	r	d	u
	b	e	a	r	a	l	u	p	e	q	m	o	c
	f	d	p	g	c	s	e	a	s	h	o	r	e

B. Which wicked witch wished which wish?

C. 1. The cheery chipmunk chases the chubby child.
   2. The sixth sheep cherishes the shiny shield.
   3. Three thin thieves stole the fifth feather from the thoughtful brother.
   4. The witty whale wonders whether the wheel will whirl round the withered wheat.
   5. We shall sew and sell sheets in the shabby shack.

D. ch: cheery ; chipmunk ; chases ; chubby ; child ; cherishes

sh: sheep ; cherishes ; shiny ; shield ; shall ; sheets ; shabby ; shack

th: the ; sixth ; three ; thin ; thieves ; fifth ; feather ; thoughtful ; brother ; whether ; withered

wh: whale ; whether ; wheel ; whirl ; wheat

3 The Tomatina – the Strangest Festival in the World

A. (Circle these words.)
food fight ; Spain ; tomatoes ; August ; festival ; Buñol ; parties ; Wednesday ; town centre

B. 1. B
2. D
3. C
4. A

C. 1. sword
2. knot
3. ghost
4. scissors
5. thumb
6. sleigh
7. palm
8. listen

D. (Individual writing of words with the same silent consonants)
1. cas(t)le
2. sta(l)k
3. (g)naw
4. t(w)o
5. autum(n)
6. (h)our
7. clim(b)
8. s(c)ience
9. (k)nigh(t)

4 Let's Save Water

A. 1. ✔
2.
3. ✔
4.
5.
6. ✔

B. (Individual writing and drawing)

C. glass ; brush ; five ; help ; save ; use ; ocean ; fish ; pot
Short Vowel: glass ; brush ; help ; fish ; pot
Long Vowel: five ; save ; use ; ocean

D.

	t	n	c	r	g	o	i	b	f		
w	b	k	q	i	v	e	s	f	r	o	g	u
c	v	z	f	x	k	i	t	e	q	m	k	d
a	l	h	l	t	l	w	b	y	w	a	z	p
k	d	x	u	a	v	s	e	o	c	r	s	m
e	p	r	t	g	x	j	l	u	p	y	t	g
p	m	y	e	z	c	w	l	h	t	d	a	u
e	u	p	l	u	g	q	o	j	a	v	p	i
	y	f	c	o	n	e	q	x	k	f	s
	n	i	r	n	b	t	h	e	l		

5 Tooth Tales from around the World

A. 1. E
2. B
3. C
4. F
5. D
6. A
7. G

B. (Colour the boxes with these words.)
toy ; brown ; join ; our ; soil ; mouth ; point ; joy ; voice ; foyer ; count ; shower ; wow

C. oi: D ; J
oy: C
ou: B ; E ; F ; H ; I
ow: A ; G ; K ; L ; M

6 Mmmmm...Poutine!

A. 1. 60
   2. Quebec
   3. cheese curds
   4. spaghetti sauce
   5. fork

B. 1. tasty
   2. eaten
   3. gooey
   4. messy

C. 1. ee
   2. oo
   3. ea
   4. ew
   5. aw
   6. ai
   7. au
   8. ay
   9. oa

D. 1. They put the poutine on the (tray)
   2. It is one of my favourite (treats)
   3. Can I have poutine on (toast)?
   4. My sister likes (plain) French fries instead.
   5. She does not like anything (gooey)

E. 1. bay ; bee ; bow ; boo
   2. pail ; peel ; pool
   3. dear ; deer ; door
   4. tray ; tree
   5. raid ; read ; reed ; road
   6. hail ; heal ; heel ; haul

7 Kelly's Broken Wrist

A. 1. helmet
   2. elbow pad
   3. wrist guard
   4. knee pad

B. 1. She fell off her bicycle.
   2. A man at the hospital took an X-ray of Kelly's wrist.
   3. She signed her name and drew a happy face on it.

C. (Circle these words.)
   park ; sport ; guard ; her ; sister ; hurt ; first

D. ar: E ; J
   er: D ; F
   ir: C ; I
   or: A ; H
   ur: B ; G

8 Onomatopoeia

A. 1. rustle
   2. quack
   3. splash
   4. buzz
   5. chime
   6. hiss
   7. chirp
   8. click
   9. rumble
   10. tinkle

B. (Circle each rhyming pair below with a different colour.)
   quack – back
   tweet – feet
   moo – shoo
   purr – fur
   say – day

C. (Individual writing of the new rhyming words)
   1. E
   2. C
   3. I
   4. G
   5. A
   6. D
   7. B
   8. J
   9. F
   10. H

9   My Special Hobby

A.

(Crossword puzzle)

1 D I F F E R E N T

2 P H O T O G R A P H S

A H O B B Y

B E N V E L O P E S

3 S P C S E N D

R E N T

S P E C I A L

B.   (Individual drawing, colouring, and writing)

C.   (Cross out these words.)
Person: Sean ; Karen
Animal: Pug ; Nemo
Place: Lake Simcoe ; Hong Kong
Thing: PlayStation ; Barbie

D.   1. My friend Tara has moved to Italy.
2. I received a Christmas card from her last Monday.
3. The stamp has a Golden Retriever on it.
4. Tara will come back to Toronto for a visit in July.

10   Berry Time

A.   1. B
2. C
3. D
4. A
5. (Individual naming and drawing of a berry)

B.   (Colour the strawberries of 2, 3, and 4.)

C.   s: baskets ; cartoons ; lollipops ; rainbows ; seasons
es: buses ; boxes ; wishes ; peaches ; benches
ies: cities ; lilies ; babies ; puppies ; butterflies

D.

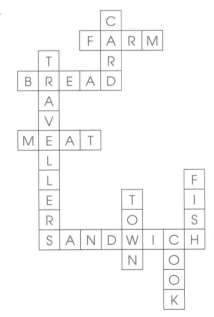

11   Who Invented the Sandwich?

A.

(Crossword puzzle)

C F A R M

T R B R E A D

A V M E A T

L L F E T I R O S S A N D W I C H N O O K

B.

1. two sandwiches

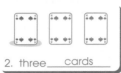

2. three cards

3. four butterflies

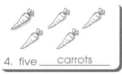

4. five carrots

5. six balls

6. seven hearts

C. (Colour the bread with these words.)
meat ; bread ; ice ; sugar ; wool ; rain ; glue

D. 1. butter
2. lollipop
3. milk
4. salt ; tea
5. dollars

12 Brother Moon and Sister Sun – an Inuit Legend

A. 1. dark
2. pulled
3. night
4. quickly
5. stayed
6. angry

B. 1. B
2. A
3. A
4. B

C. (Colour the suns of 1, 2, 7, and 9.)

D. 1. The sun is shining brightly.
2. We cannot look at the sun directly. /
We cannot look directly at the sun.
3. We can see the full moon tonight.
4. It is like a shiny, round mirror.

E. (Individual writing)

13 Chinese Birth Signs

A. 1. Rat
2. Ox
3. Tiger
4. Rabbit
5. Dragon
6. Snake
7. Horse
8. Sheep
9. Monkey
10. Rooster
11. Dog
12. Pig

B. 1. Do
2. which
3. Does
4. How
5. Is
6. What
7. Are
8. Why
9. When

C. 1. Can you draw your birth sign?
2. Where can we learn about horoscopes?
3. Do horoscopes really tell us our future?

D. 1. Which birth sign comes after Rabbit? /
Which birth sign does Dragon come after?
2. Is Rat the first birth sign on the list?
3. What animal would you like to add to the list?

14 Billy's Bad Dream

A. 1. A
    2. B
    3. B
    4. B
B. (Write 2, 3, 5, 6, and 8 in the bag.)
C. 1. A
    2. C
    3. D
    4. B
D. (Individual writing)

15 S'mores!

A.

B. 1. Put a chocolate square on a graham cracker.
    2. Heat a marshmallow over a campfire.
    3. Place the marshmallow on the chocolate square.
    4. Put another graham cracker on top.
    5. Enjoy the s'more!
C. 1.
    2. ✔
    3. ✔
    4. ✔
    5. ✔
    6.
    7.
    8.
    9. ✔
D. 1. Turn down the volume.
    2. Put away your books.
    3. Just leave it there, Cedric.
    4. Don't throw it away.

E. (Suggested answers)
    1. Feed the fish, Jane.
    2. Meet me at the theatre.
    3. Don't ride your bike on the road.

16 How Canada Got Its Name

A. Canada: B
    China: D
    Japan: A
    Namibia: C
B. (Colour the maple leaves of 1, 2, and 4.)
C. 1. name
    2. Canada
    3. People
    4. beaver
    5. Ottawa
    6. tulips
    7. Tourists
    8. summer
D. 1. My family <u>came to Canada five years ago</u>.
    2. We <u>lived in Montreal at first</u>.
    3. We <u>moved here last year</u>.
    4. I <u>go to Westland School</u>.
    5. I <u>have made many new friends</u>.
    6. I <u>always send e-mail to my friends in Montreal</u>.
    7. I <u>miss them</u>.
    8. Dennis <u>said he might come to visit me this summer</u>.

17 Scotty the T. Rex

A. Paragraph One: A
    Paragraph Two: B
    Paragraph Three: B
B. 1. ?
    2. .
    3. !
    4. ?
    5. .
    6. .
    7. ?
    8. .
    9. !

C. 1. You can go to Marineland in these months: July, August, and September.
2. We fed fish, deer, and killer whales in Marineland.
3. Dolphins, walruses, and sea lions performed in the shows.
4. We had salad, steak, cheesecake, and tea for dinner.
5. You need these to make the drink: soda, coconut milk, and pineapple juice.
6. There are four main characters in the story. They are Celia, Lester, Robert, and Tommy.
7. Chips, lollipops, ice cream, and chocolates are all my favourite treats.

18 My Little Sister's Challenge

A. 1. challenge
2. happened
3. scared
4. cheered
B. 1. two-and-a-half years old
2. using the toilet instead of diapers
3. scared
4. very proud
C. we: C
they: E
he: D
she: A
it: B
D. 1. I
2. He
3. you
4. They
E. 1. us
2. me
3. them
4. her
5. it
6. him
7. you

19 Canada's Great Polar Bear Swim

A. 1. celebrate
2. northern
3. swimmers
4. party
B. 1. It is held on New Year's Day.
2. It is held in English Bay in Vancouver.
3. It was first held in 1920.
4. More than 2000 swimmers enter the event now.
C.

s	f	w	o	z	k	x	m	u	r	p	e	i	t	h
b	r	h	v	e	g	a	d	o	e	s	y	c	t	n
i	c	o	m	e	s	o	e	s	a	x	m	s	h	e
p	t	s	g	d	j	c	n	l	c	i	b	u	i	q
e	n	t	y	v	h	w	a	s	h	e	s	g	n	j
s	z	s	l	a	x	e	j	w	e	q	m	t	k	u
c	e	l	e	b	r	a	t	e	s	z	d	j	s	m
e	y	i	r	h	v	r	w	p	g	u	r	a	k	p
k	d	l	c	s	o	s	b	f	q	h	o	l	d	s

D. 1. The club organizes the event.
2. Many members join the Polar Bear Swim.
3. ✔
4. I want to join the swim this year.
5. My friend Celia swims every day.
6. ✔

20 Why the Sea Is Salty

A. (Colour these pictures.)
1. B
2. A
3. A
4. A
5. B

B.

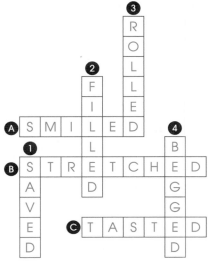

C. 1. lived
2. rained
3. rushed
4. stopped
5. helped
D. She chopped some potatoes and carrots and added them to the soup. After about an hour, she sprinkled some salt in the soup. Then she ladled the soup into bowls. We all enjoyed the soup.

21 My Grandma's Special Hobby

A. 1. ✔
2. ✔
3.
4. ✔
5. ✔
6.
B. (Individual drawing and writing)
C. 1. is
2. is
3. are
4. are
5. is
6. am
7. is

D. 1. is showing
2. am making
3. are playing
4. are doing
5. are fishing
6. are learning
7. is shutting
8. is running

22 Fluffy the Wonder Dog

A. 1. special
2. while
3. slide
4. morning
5. ladder
6. paper
7. climbed
8. mouth
9. laughed
10. reminded
B. 1. was
2. was ; were
3. was
4. was
5. was
6. were
7. were
C. 1. were
2. having
3. ✔
4. cycling
5. ✔
6. was

23 A New Student in Class

A. 1. sad
2. angry
3. jealous
4. happy
5. lonely
6. ashamed

B.   1. ✔
     2.
     3.
     4.
     5. ✔
C.   (Circle these words.)
     old ; nice ; good ; three ; violet ; round ; twelve ;
     scared ; square

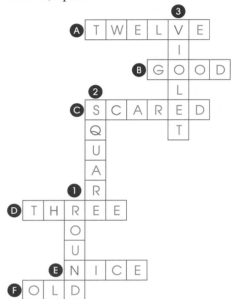

D.   (Individual writing and drawing)
E.   1. red
     2. delicious
     3. five
     4. crazy
     5. favourite
     6. round

24 A New Game

A.   3 ; 2 ; 4 ; 1 ; 6 ; 5
B.   1. Y
     2. Y
     3. N
     4. N
     5. N

C.   (Individual drawing and colouring)
D.   at: D ; E
     on: B
     in: A ; C ; F
E.   (Individual writing)

25 I Want to Be a...

A.   1. ✔
     2. ✔
     3.
     4. ✔
     5. ✔
     6.
     7. ✔
     8. ✔
B.   (Individual drawing and writing)
C.   1.
     2.
     3.
     4.
     5.
D.   1. I need bread, ham,^and cheese to make the
        sandwich.
     2. You can pick only one, the one with the
        bunny^or the one with the bear.
     3. We can keep this ending^or write a new ending
        to our play.
     4. The play was great^but the ending was too sad.
E.   1. I don't like sweet things but this dessert is
        delicious.
     2. My family is going on a trip and Sally is joining
        us.
     3. We can meet at the theatre or I can pick you
        up.

26 When Grandma Was a Girl Like Me

A. (Individual drawing, writing, and colouring)
B. 1.
    2. ✔
    3. ✔
    4.
    5. ✔
C. 1. smart
    2. damp
    3. dawn
    4. cheerful
    5. small
    6. fast
    7. arrive
    8. light
D.

r	i	s	w	r	o	n	g	h	
r	d	o	h	l	f	a	l	l	u	c
m	i	q	a	o	f	y	v	e	x	g	k	u
t	g	c	h	r	r	d	i	m	g	e	j	o
i	h	o	v	t	d	z	b	w	m	h	t	l
n	t	n	c	l	u	t	i	n	y	a	p	d
d	n	t	o	u	t	s	i	d	e	q	a	f
o	k	i	i	l	e	n	g	t	h	y	u	n
o	c	n	s	j	p	q	b	o	a	z	s	l
r	z	u	d	w	a	j	r	x	s	g	e	e
s	p	e	r	m	g	y	i	e	c	w	b	x
	u	n	u	s	e	d	g	p	e	h	v	
		l	r	f	s	k	h	i	n	u		
			o	t	b	n	t	s	d			

27 The Fox and the Stork

A. 4 ; 1 ; 5 ; 3 ; 6 ; 2
B. 1. den
    2. invited
    3. shallow

4. licked
5. beak
6. jars
C. 1. The fox is ^not adding salt to the soup.
    2. The soup is ^not boiling.
    3. It is ^not very hot.
    4. The bowls are ^not big.
    5. They are ^not made of clay.
    6. I am ^not hungry.
    7. I am ^not drinking the soup.
    8. They are ^not washing the dishes.
D. 1. does not mind
    2. does not have
    3. do not go
    4. do not ride
    5. do not need
    6. does not hide

28 Johnny Appleseed

A. 1. John Chapman
    2. United States
    3. apple trees
    4. Ohio River
    5. gentle
    6. friends
    7. storyteller

l	h	a	v	j	r	m			
e	p	d	O	p	U	o	s	a	g	k
s	c	a	p	p	l	e		t	r	e	e	s
n	j		m	f	i	g	R	a		n	C	j
b	s	t	o	r	y	t	e	l	l	e	r	d
t	g	O	h	i	o		R	i	v	e	r	n
U	n	i	t	e	d		S	t	a	t	e	s
w	J	o	h	n		C	h	a	p	m	a	n
o	l	U	p	d	a	q	O	e	j	c	i	f
k	b	h	s	f	g	e	n	t	l	e		

B. 1. E ; B ; D ; C ; A
    2. B ; E ; C ; A ; D
C. (Individual writing)
    1. B   2. C
    3. D   4. A
    5. E   6. F

1 My Family

A. (Individual picture and answers)
B. (Individual drawing and answers)

2 Different Traditions and Celebrations

A. 1. A
   2. C
   3. B
   4. D
B. (Individual writing)

3 Traditional Foods

A. 1. oliebollen ; the Netherlands
   2. gnocchi ; Italy
   3. turnip cake ; China
B. (Individual drawing and answers)

4 Our Traditions and Celebrations

A. 1. Indian   2. November
   3. five-day   4. candles
   5. Lights   6. Kheer
B. A
C.

Festival	Diwali	Hanukkah
Another Name	Festival of Lights	Festival of Lights
Celebrated by	Indians	Jews
Things People Do	decorate homes with lamps and candles	light candles in a Menorah for eight days
Foods People Eat	kheer and coconut sweets	latkes and sufganiyot

5 Ethnic Foods and Things

A. 1. D
   2. A
   3. B
   4. C
B. (Individual drawings and answers)

6 Special Days

A. 1. July 1   2. birthday
   3. fireworks   4. flag
   5. November 11   6. poppies
   7. soldiers
B. Iranian Canadians: A ; C ; D ; G
   Chinese Canadians: B ; E ; F

7 Changing Traditions

A. (Individual answers)

8 Celebrating Differently

A. (Individual colouring)
    1. candles
    2. feast
    3. gifts
    (Individual answer)
B. (Individual drawings)

9 Mapping Our Traditions

A. 1. Algonquin ; Ojibwe ;
       Timmins
    2. Huron and Petun
B. 1. ancestors
    2. north
    3. year
    4. dance
    5. culture
    6. Canada

10 Our Thanksgiving Celebration

A. 1. thanks
    2. ceremony
    3. explorer
    4. harvest
    5. turkeys
    6. cranberry
B. Food: turkey ; maple syrup ; cranberry sauce ;
    squash and corn
    How to Get It?: catch ; from maple trees ; cook ;
    gather
    (Individual writing)

11 Our World

A. The Seven Continents — Asia ; South America ; North America ; Africa ; Europe ; Antarctica ; Australia

B.
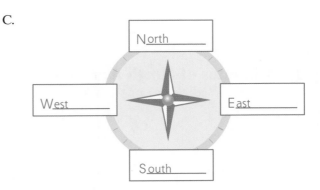

C.

1. north

2. east

12 The Globe

A. 1. the Equator
    2. Northern Hemisphere
    3. Southern Hemisphere
    4. North Pole
    5. South Pole
B. 1. rain
    2. rainforests
    3. Brazil
    4. north
    5. water
    6. Canada
    7. south
    8. land
    9. Chile
    10. ice
    11. polar bear
    12. snows
    13. penguin

13 Climates of North America

A.

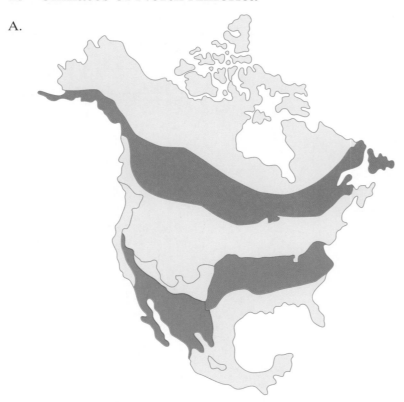

Canada ; the United States ; Mexico ; Mexico ;
Canada

B. warmer ; colder ; seasons
    1. summer
    2. spring
    3. winter
    4. fall

14 Unique Countries

A. 1. Southern
    2. south
    3. Equator
    4. warm
    5. Amazon
    6. rainforest
B. Northern ; east ; far ; cold
    1. hot springs
    2. glacier
    3. volcano
    4. geyser

15 Our Unique Country

A. 1. C
   2. D
   3. A
   4. B
B. 1. stores
   2. necessities
   3. transportation
   4. recreational
   5. hiking
   6. skiing
C. (Individual answers)

16 Travel around the World

A. 1. Thailand
   2. China
   3. Mali
   4. Japan
B. Savannah: grassland ; trees ; graze ; C ; F
   Rainforest: rain ; forest ; wildlife ; B ; D
   Desert: rain ; sand ; plants ; A ; E

17 Our Basic Needs

A. (Individual answers)
B. 1. mule ; U.S.A.
   2. subway ; France
   3. scooter ; Taiwan

18 Living around the World

A.

B. 1. meat ; milk
   2. seals ; food
   3. bakery
   4. rice ; fish

19 Clothes and Homes

A. 1. Delhi, India
   2. Lima, Peru
   3. Nairobi, Kenya
   4. Nunavut, Canada
B. 1. mud brick
   2. snow block
   3. cob
   4. igloo
   5. cob house
   6. adobe house

21 Foods from around the World

A. oranges: Florida
   tomatoes: California
   kiwis: New Zealand
   (Individual answers)
B. 1. They are located near the Equator.
   2. Countries near the Equator have warm climates, which allow food crops to grow.
   3. hot ; bananas ; soil

20 Sports and Recreation

A.

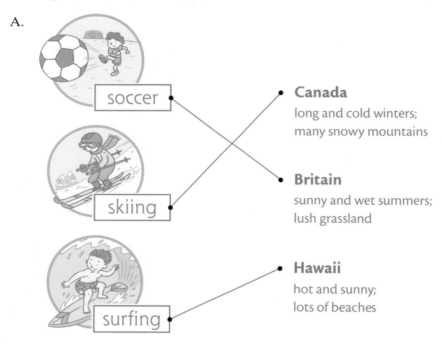

soccer — Britain
skiing — Canada
surfing — Hawaii

Canada
long and cold winters;
many snowy mountains

Britain
sunny and wet summers;
lush grassland

Hawaii
hot and sunny;
lots of beaches

B. British Columbia: B ; D
   Quebec: C ; E
   Lake Ontario: A ; G
   Alberta: F ; H

22 Where People Live

A. 1. Toronto
    2. Montreal
    3. Calgary
    Ontario

B.

1. Most of the larger cities in Canada are in Southern Canada, specifically Ontario.
2. (Suggested answer)
Most people want to live in cities, rather than in rural areas. It is also because the southern part is warmer.

23 Adapting to a Place

A. 1. A
    2. C
    3. B
B. Managua, Nicaragua: A, D, E, I, L
Florida, U.S.A.: B, C, J, M
The Arctic: F, G, H, K, N, O

24 Preserving Our Resources

A. (Suggested answers)
    1. a. North America
       b. Asia
       c. Africa
    2. We need it for drinking.
    3. (Suggested answer)
       Turn off the tap when brushing my teeth.
B. A: grow own food
    B: save electricity
    C: destroy forests
    (Suggested answer)
    C does not save our resources because it is getting rid of trees, which are important for people and animals. People need it for fresh air and animals need it for shelter.

1 Animals

A. • have fur or hair

• give birth to live babies

• feed its babies milk

B. 1. Reptiles ; alligator, turtle
2. Birds ; parrot, robin
3. Amphibians ; toad, salamander
4. Fish ; goldfish, shark

2 Ways Animals Eat and Move

A. 1. C   2. A
3. D   4. B
B. 1.

2.

C. 1. a human
2. a duck
3. a bird
4. a snake
5. a fish

3 Animal Homes

A. 1. predator
2. sun
3. cold
4. predator
B. 1. warren
2. den
3. roost
4. hive
5. web
6. lodge
C. 1. B
2. C
3. A

4 Winter Survival

A. 1. slow ;

2. feathers ;

3. fur ;

4. nuts ;

B. 1. B
2. A
3. A
C.

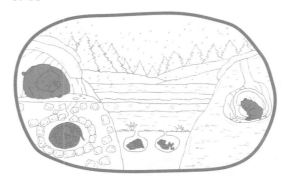

5 Migration

A.

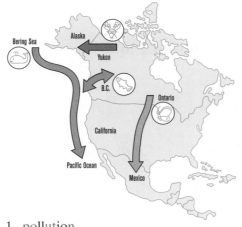

B. 1. pollution
   2. hunters
   3. storms
   4. predators

C.

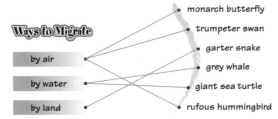

6 Animal Babies

A.

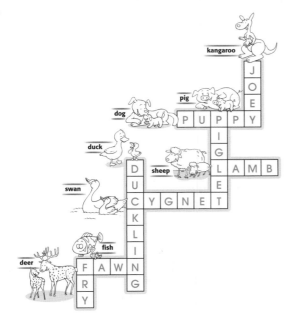

B. 1. B
   2. C
   3. A
C. 1. A
   2. D
   3. C
   4. B

7 Animal Growth

A. 1. 2 ; 1 ; 3
   2. 3 ; 1 ; 2
   3. 2 ; 3 ; 1
B. reddish brown
   bluish grey
   white
C. 1. a mouse
   2. a harp seal
   3. a bird

8 Life Cycles

A. Frog: egg ; tadpole ; adult
   Dragonfly: egg ; larva ; adult
   Butterfly: egg ; caterpillar ; chrysalis ; adult

B.

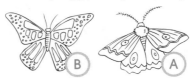

C.

9 Camouflage and Adaptation

A. (Colour these animals.)
1. tiger ; snake
2. camel ; hairy desert scorpion
3. polar bear ; arctic fox

B. 1.

2.

C. 1. predator
2. prey
3. predator

10 Properties of Liquids and Solids

A.

B.

C.

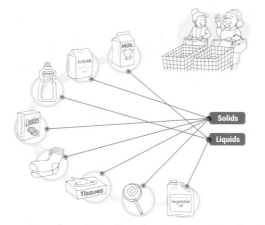

D. 1. liquid
2. solid

11 More about Liquids and Solids

A. 1 ; 3
B.

C.

D. 1. absorbs
2. dissolves

12 Three States of Water

A. 1. gas
2. liquid
3. solid
4. liquid
5. liquid
6. gas
7. solid
8. solid

B. 1. melt
2. freeze
3. evaporate

C.

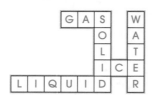

13 Buoyancy

A.

B. 1. wood
    2. metal

C.

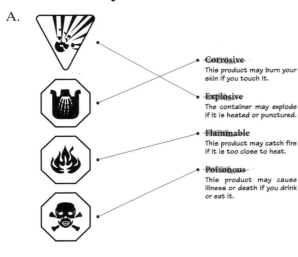

14 Hazard Symbols

A.

Corrosive
This product may burn your skin if you touch it.

Explosive
The container may explode if it is heated or punctured.

Flammable
This product may catch fire if it is too close to heat.

Poisonous
This product may cause illness or death if you drink or eat it.

B. 1. A
    2. C
    3. B
    4. D

C.

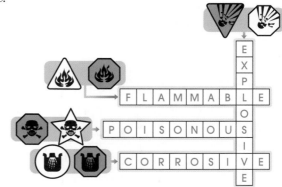

15 Air around Us

A. 1.

2.

B.

e	S	t			A	z	u	h	i	S	X
b	r	e	e	z	e	h	a	f	a	g
	k	l	P	q	p	w	r	e	n	c
m	g	a	l	e	h	r	m	Y	t	h
o	n	d	z	a	y		a	o	a	i
n	f	g	j	k	r	l	t	E		n
s	i	r	o	c	c	o	t	a	A	o
o	w	e	w	i	n	d	a	y	n	o
o	S	w		A	j	k	n	D	a	k
n	t	y	W	p	s	i	m	o	o	m
a	s	w	i	l	l	i	w	a	w	v

C. (Individual answers)

16 Water around Us

A. 1. river
2. waterfall
3. lake
4. pond
5. underground
6. ocean
7. ice

B.

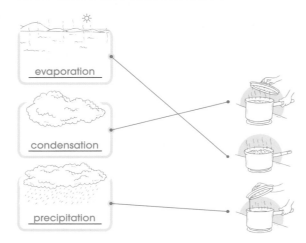

C.

evaporation

condensation

precipitation

17 Clean Air and Water

A.

B. 1.

2.

3.

4.

18 Energy Input and Output

A. 1. output ; The bell rings.
2. output ; The toy moves. ;
input ; Wind up the toy.
3. input ; Press the switch. ;
output ; The light turns on.

B.

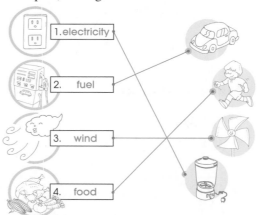

1. electricity
2. fuel
3. wind
4. food

C. input, output, movement, food, electricity, fuel, wind

19 Energy from Moving Water and Wind

A. 1. w ; C
   2. k ; D
   3. s ; B
   4. r ; A
B. 1. C
   2. D
   3. B
   4. A
C. r ; n ; a

20 Windmills and Water Wheels

A. 1. Wind
   2. boats
   3. windmills
   4. corn
   5. water
   6. saws
   7. electricity
B. 1. moving water
   2. moving water
   3. moving water
   4. wind
   5. No energy can be produced.

21 Positions

A.

B. behind, in front of, above, in, under, over, beside, on, between

C.

22 Movements

A. 1. turning
   2. sliding
   3. bouncing
   4. rolling
   5. zigzagging
   6. swinging
   7. spinning
B. 1. E
   2. A
   3. D
   4. B
   5. C
C. 1. slide
   2. turn
   3. roll

23 Simple Machines

A. A: screw
   B: wedge
   C: lever
   D: wheel and axle
   E: pulley
   F: inclined plane
   1. B
   2. D
   3. A
   4. F
   5. E
   6. C

B.

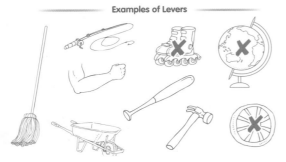

Examples of Levers

C. 1. wedges
   2. wheels and axles
   3. levers

24 Movements and Mechanisms

A. 1. turning ; swinging
   2. vibrating ; turning
   3. bouncing ; vibrating
   4. vibrating ; spinning

B.

C. 1. wedge ; pushing
   2. wedge ; turning
   3. screw ; pulling